Die KOMPASS-Wanderkarte 1:25 (
der Darstellung des hochalpinen R;
rismusort Mayrhofen ist. Hier verei
täler des Zillertales zum breiten H;
Richtung dem Inntal zustrebt, wobe
das von Osten mündende, wasserr
sogenannten „Inneren Gründe", verr
tem Rund das Hintere Zillertal umsc
henden Gründe eignen sich vortrefflicn tur Wanderungen zu den im Talschluss liegenden
geräumigen Hütten des Alpenvereins. Östlich von Mayrhofen betritt man den Zillergrund (Ta-
xibusverbindung), der sich wieder in das Zillergründl, den Hundskehlgrund und Sundergrund gliedert. Südlich erreicht man über eine Talstufe den Stillupgrund (Mautstraße zum
Stausee). Bei Ginzling führt der Floitengrund in das Herz der Zillertaler Alpen. Gunggl,
Zemmgrund und Schlegeisgrund reihen sich aneinander, ehe der Zamser Grund zum Pfitscher Joch, 2248 m, und damit an die Grenze zu Südtirol/Italien hinaufführt. Zwischen dem
Zamser und dem Tuxer Tal erhebt sich der Tuxer Hauptkamm, mit dem Olperer, 3476 m,
wohl eine der markantesten Gipfelgestalten östlich des Brenners, die weithin sichtbar ist.
Von Finkenberg eröffnet das Tuxer Tal den Zugang in die Tuxer Alpen und zum Ganzjahres-
skigebiet am Tuxer Ferner. Über den Gerlospass, 1531 m, kommt man auf zwei Wegen nach
Wald im Pinzgau im oberen Salzachtal: entweder auf der aussichtsreichen Mautstraße (Blick
auf die weltberühmten Krimmler Wasserfälle) über Krimml oder auf der mautfreien Straße
über das Almdorf Königsleiten.

Geologie

Die Schönheit der Zillertaler Alpen mit dem Tuxer und Zillertaler Hauptkamm und der Reichenspitzgruppe beruht auf den kühnen Formen der dunklen Grate und Gipfel, die in schar-
fen Kontrasten zu den gleißenden Firnen der „Keese" (= Gletscher) stehen, von denen
schäumende Bäche in die engen, tief ausgeschürften Täler stürzen. Ein völlig anderes Landschaftsbild finden wir dagegen in den im Norden anschließenden, unvergletscherten Tuxer
Alpen. Dieser Gegensatz beruht auf dem geologischen Bau des Gebirges, der folgende, im
allgemeinen von West nach Ost verlaufende Einheiten unterscheiden lässt. Der Kern der Zillertaler Alpen baut sich hauptsächlich aus harten Gneisen auf. Diese Zentralgneiszone beginnt im Westen mit den beiden Ästen des Tuxer und Zillertaler Hauptkammes, welche in
der Stillupe zu einer einheitlichen Masse verschmelzen, die sich ostwärts bis in die Hohen
Tauern fortsetzt. Die Südgrenze dieser Zone verläuft durch das Südtiroler Ahrntal und zieht
von diesem zum Eisbruggjoch nach Westen. Im Norden wird sie durch die Linie Kraxentrager – Kaserer – Mayrhofen – Krimml begrenzt. Der Gneiskern wird beiderseits von einer
Schieferhülle umschlossen, die im Westen auch zwischen die Gneisäste eingreift. Ihre
Nordgrenze zieht nahe dem nördlichen Kartenrand von Matrei im Wipptal über Hippach zum
Gerlospass. Die Hülle setzt sich aus verschiedenartigsten Gesteinen, vorwiegend kristalli-
nen Schiefern, zusammen und wird in eine untere, dem Zentralgneis näher liegende Zone
mit vorwiegend kalkfreien und kalkarmen Gesteinen und in eine obere, außen liegende Zone, in der auch kalkreiche Gesteine stark vertreten sind, gegliedert. Den Bergwanderer er-
reut der Reichtum an schönen Mineralien, unter denen besonders die Granate, die am
Rossrugg gesammelt und in einer kleinen Granatmühle am Bach unterhalb der Berliner Hütte gepocht wurden, bekannt sind. Im Bereich der harten, widerstandsfähigen Gneise schuf
die Erosion kühne Gipfelformen und scharfe Grate, die auch zur Zeit der höchsten Vereisung
aus den mächtigen Eismassen, die die Täler erfüllten und in den Tuxer Alpen auch die Gip-
felregionen überfluteten und abhobelten, herausragten. Die Eisströme haben die Täler tief
ausgeschnitten zu jener typischen Talform, für die die Glaziologen hier in den Zillertaler Al-

pen, einem ihrer ältesten Forschungsgebiete im alpinen Raum, den Ausdruck „Trogtal" präg-
ten. Die weiten Kare der Nordseite bilden auch noch die Nährgebiete mächtiger Gletscher,
die als natürliche Wasserspeicher große Bedeutung für die Energiewirtschaft besitzen. Am
ungemein steilen Südabfall des Gebirges konnten sich dagegen nur kleinere Gletscher entwickeln. An den Hängen und in den Talsohlen lagerte sich Verwitterungsmaterial in großen
Mengen ab, das durch die wasserreichen Bäche weitertransportiert wird. Mur- und Über-
schwemmungskatastrophen suchten das Zillertal immer wieder schwer heim. Durch die Errichtung von drei großen Speicherbecken (Schlegeis, Stillup und Zillergründl) können die
Hochwasserkatastrophen mittlerweile unter Kontrolle gehalten werden.

Siedlungsgeschichte

Politisch gehört das dargestellte Gebiet bis zur Staatsgrenze gegen Italien zum Nordtiroler
Bezirk Schwaz. Nur im Westen reicht die Gemeinde Schmirn des Bezirkes Innsbruck-Land
herein, seit 1926 allerdings nur mehr bis zum Tuxer Joch. Im Südwesten verlor die Gemeinde St. Jakob in Pfitsch des Bezirkes Sterzing nach dem Ersten Weltkrieg ihr Gebiet
nördlich des Pfitscher Joches. Das Ahrntal wird zur Pustertaler Talschaft mit dem Mittelpunkt Bruneck gerechnet. Dass von ihm seit je enge Beziehungen über das Hörndljoch,
Hundskehljoch und Heilig-Geist-Jöchl zum inneren Zillergrund und seinen Nebentälern be-
standen, beweist die Tatsache, dass die Almen dieser Gebiete noch heute den Ahrntaler
Bauern gehören, während sie politisch und steuerlich schon früh mit dem Zillertal verbunden waren. Dass der einzige vorgeschichtliche Fund des Gebietes, eine Bronzenadel, am
Tuxer Joch gemacht wurde, scheint dafür auch bezeichnend, besitzt aber wohl doch zu ge-
ringe Beweiskraft. Der östliche Abschnitt der Karte mit Krimml ist dem Salzburger Bezirk
Zell am See zugehörig.
Die Ortsnamenforschung ergab, dass auch das Zillertal von später romanisierten Illyrern
besiedelt wurde. Diese wohl nur dünne Bevölkerungsschicht wurde jedoch von den baju-
warischen Siedlern, die ab dem 6. Jahrhundert eindrangen, vollständig aufgesaugt. Dass
die Bayern die Hauptsiedlungsarbeit leisteten, geht aus den zahlreichen auf Rodungstätigkeit hinweisenden Siedlungs- und Flurnamen hervor. Schriftlich wurde das Zillertal erst in
einer Urkunde vom Jahr 889 erwähnt, laut welcher König Arnulf, der zugleich Herzog von
Bayern war, Pilgrim, dem späteren Erzbischof von Salzburg, bedeutenden Grundbesitz im
„Cilarestal" übertrug. Grundherrschaft und Graftschaftsgewalt deckten sich hier jedoch
nicht. Der Ziller bildete zur Römerzeit die Grenze zwischen Rätien und Norikum und ist seit
ältester Zeit die Grenze zwischen zwei Grafschaften. Die westlich des Flusses unterstand
nachweislich seit dem 11. Jahrhundert den Bischöfen von Brixen und ging von diesen an
die Grafen von Andechs, nach deren Aussterben an die Hirschberger und 1263 bzw. 1282
schließlich an die Grafen von Tirol über. Den östlichen Teil dieser Grafschaft verliehen schon
die Andechser an ihre Dienstmannen, die Herren von Rottenburg, deren Stammburg bei
Jenbach stand. Daraus entwickelte sich das Landgericht Rottenburg, das bis zu seiner Ost-
grenze am Ziller die volle Gerichtsbarkeit ausübte. Östlich des Flusses reichte eine eigene
Grafschaft bis Kufstein und Erl, als deren Inhaber das bayrische Grafengeschlecht der Rapotonen, die Bischöfe von Regensburg und seit 1205 die Wittelsbacher genannt werden.
Aus deren „Grafschaft im Gebirge" entwickelten sich die Landgerichte Kufstein, Kitzbühel
und Rattenberg. Letzteres übte bis zum Ziller die hohe Gerichtsbarkeit aus. Von 1290 – 1380
unterstand es als Pfand den Tiroler Landesherren, die es zusammen mit Kitzbühel und Kufstein durch Kaiser Maximilian I. 1504 endgültig erwerben konnten. Es gelang jedoch den
Erzbischöfen von Salzburg ihre Besitzungen im Zillertal fast vollkommen auszubauen.
Schon im 12. Jahrhundert schufen sie zur Verwaltung ihres Besitzes im Zillertal ein eige-
nes Amt und etwa seit 1200 übten sie die Vogteirechte selbst aus. Ende des 13. Jahrhunderts bauten sie zum Schutz am Eingang des Tales die Burg Kropfsberg, deren Pfleger hin-
fort der erste Beamte des Erzbischofs für das Zillertal war.

Durch die enge Verzahnung der Besitzungen und Rechte kam es im Laufe der Jahrhunderte immer wieder zu Streitigkeiten zwischen Salzburg und Tirol. Die Tiroler Landesfürsten beanspruchten nämlich aufgrund ihrer alten Grafschaftsrechte nicht nur die Blutgerichtsbarkeit in den aus diesen Grafschaften hervorgegangenen Gerichtssprengeln, sondern auch die wirtschaftlich bedeutenden Forst-, Jagd- und Bergregale. Tatsächlich übten jedoch die Erzbischöfe von Salzburg in ihren Grundherrschaften beiderseits des Zillers fast die gesamten Hoheitsrechte aus, mit Ausnahme der hohen Blutgerichtsbarkeit, wobei allerdings die Zuständigkeit der Landgerichte Rottenburg und Rattenberg von den Salzburger Beamten immer wieder übergangen wurde. Hinsichtlich der Nutzung der Regale gelang es den Tirolern, ihre Ansprüche wenigstens teilweise durchzusetzen. Als im Jahr 1803 alle geistlichen Fürstentümer Deutschlands säkularisiert wurden, ging das Erzbistum Salzburg an das Haus Habsburg über und zwar zunächst an die Nebenlinie Toscana und erst 1805 direkt an das Kaiserreich Österreich. Gleichzeitig wurde allerdings durch die Abtretung Tirols dessen Anteil am Zillertal bayrisch, wodurch der alte Kampf um die Hoheitsrechte nun mit gewechselten Rollen weiter ausgefochten wurde. Am Tiroler Freiheitskampf 1809 beteiligten sich auch die ehemals salzburgischen Gemeinden aus eigenem Antrieb. Andreas Hofer schloss mit ihnen eine Vereinbarung, wonach das ganze Zillertal mit dem Land Tirol vereinigt werden sollte. Dieser Zusammenschluss erfolgte dann allerdings unter bayrischer Oberhoheit, da Österreich nach seiner Niederlage auch Salzburg an Bayern abtreten musste. Diese Regelung war jedoch nur von kurzer Dauer, da Bayern nach dem Wiener Kongreß seine Erwerbungen insgesamt wieder an Österreich zurückgeben musste. Das salzburgische Zillertal und Brixental wurden 1816 auf Anordnung von Kaiser Franz I. endgültig mit dem Land Tirol vereinigt, was von der Bevölkerung, die sich offenbar immer als zusammengehörig fühlte, freudig aufgenommen wurde. In kirchlicher Hinsicht blieb jedoch die alte Zweiteilung bis zum heutigen Tag erhalten. Noch immer bildet der Ziller die Bistumsgrenze. Die Pfarren rechts des Flusses mit den grünen Kirchtürmen (Dekanat Zell am Ziller) gehören zur Diözese Salzburg, die auf der linken Flussseite mit den roten Kirchtürmen (Dekanat Fügen) gehören zur Diözese Innsbruck.

Ungünstige Umstände führten die Menschen früh aus dem Tal, da dessen bäuerliche Lebensgrundlage mit zunehmender Bevölkerung zu bescheiden wurde. Händler aus dem Zil-

Bauernhöfe/Farmsteads/masi in/a Gemais

Junger Bub in der Tuxer Tracht/All dressed up in Tux
Ragazzo nel costume tradizionale di Tux

lertal zogen als Hausierer landauf und landab. Setzte man ursprünglich, d.h. nachweislich schon im 16. Jahrhundert, vor allem überschüssige landwirtschaftliche Produkte wie Schmalz, Käse und Vieh in den Nachbargebieten ab, so weitete sich der Handel allmählich auch auf andere Waren aus. Beliebt waren seit je der echte Zillertaler Schnaps, mit dessen Herstellung und Vertrieb Wurzelgräber, Brenner und Händler beschäftigt waren. Besonders bekannt waren die Zillertaler Handschuhhändler, deren Waren zumeist nicht im Tal selbst hergestellt wurden. Im 17. und 18. Jahrhundert trieben die „Ölträger" mit allerlei Salben, Ölen und Tinkturen für Mensch und Vieh einen schwunghaften Handel, wobei die Käufer allerdings vielfach mit reinen Quacksalbereien richtiggehend „angeschmiert" wurden.

Die Unbeugsamkeit in Gewissens- und Religionsfragen führte 1837 über 400 Menschen, vorwiegend aus den Gemeinden des inneren Tales Finkenberg und Brandberg, aus der Heimat, da der Tiroler Landtag das Toleranzpatent von Josef II. nicht anerkennen wollte. Die Auswanderer konnten sich in Preußisch-Schlesien geschlossen ansiedeln und das von ihnen aufgebaute Dorf „Zillertal" verkörperte bis zur neuerlichen Vertreibung 1945 ein Stück Tiroler Heimat. Die standhafte Haltung dieser Auswanderer fand in ganz Europa Bewunderer und trug zum Bekanntwerden des Tales bei. Insbesondere warben aber seit ca. 1820 Sängergruppen und -familien wie die Rainer, Leo, Strasser und Hollaus in ganz Europa für ihr schönes Tal, das schon damals für den Fremdenverkehr entdeckt wurde. Dieser nahm dann vor allem ab ca. 1850 mit dem Erwachen des Alpinismus und der Erschließung des Gebirges bedeutend zu und bildet heute neben der Landwirtschaft die Hauptgrundlage der Wirtschaft. Die Industrie fehlt im ganzen Tal, nur in den großen Talorten entwickeln sich in jüngster Zeit einige größere Gewerbebetriebe sehr gut, doch ohne das Landschaftsbild zu sehr zu beeinträchtigen. Starke Eingriffe in dieses gingen dagegen vom Kraftwerksbau aus, durch den die davon betroffenen Gründe ihre bisherige Unberührtheit verloren. Neue Attraktionen entstanden durch die Stauseen Schlegeis, Stillup und Zillergründl.

Der früher weitverbreitete Bergbau ist heute vollständig erloschen. Das Goldbergwerk am Hainzenberg wurde bis in die zweite Hälfte des 19. Jahrhunderts betrieben (heute Schaubergwerk). Das Granatvorkommen am Rossrugg wurde Mitte des 18. Jahrhunderts von einem wildernden Bauern entdeckt. Daraufhin wurden die schönen Steine fast 100 Jahre lang planmäßig gesammelt und in einer Granatstampfe im Zemmgrund gesäubert und an böhmische Schleifereien verkauft. 1836 wurde der Betrieb eingestellt. Nur der alte Kupferbergbau bei Prettau im Ahrntal wurde von 1959 bis 1971 in bescheidenem Umfang wieder aufgenommen (heute Südtiroler Bergbaumuseum/Besucherbergwerk Prettau). Neu erschlossen wurden nach dem Ersten Weltkrieg die Magnesit- und Scheelitvorkommen oberhalb von Lanersbach, durch deren Abbau und Aufbereitung einige hundert Arbeitskräfte bis zur Schließung im Jahr 1976 beschäftigt wurden.

Die schmucke Tracht – schwarzes Samtmieder mit hellem Seidentuch und ebensolcher Schürze zum schwarzen Rock für Mädchen und Frauen, schwarzlederne Kniehose und grauer Lodenjanker mit schwarzem Besatz über weißem Hemd und rotem Brustfleck für die Männer, dazu für beide Geschlechter der schwarze Hut mit Goldquaste – wird bei weltlichen und kirchlichen Festen noch häufig getragen.

Tier- und Pflanzenwelt

Die Jagdleidenschaft steckt den Zillertalern im Blut. Ihr fiel das einst in den inneren Gründen weitverbreitete Steinwild vollständig zum Opfer, die letzten Steinböcke ließ der Erzbischof von Salzburg Anfang des 18. Jahrhunderts aussiedeln. Dagegen ist der Bestand an Gamswild noch gut. Hirsche gibt es vor allem in der Gerlos in großer Zahl, wo man das Wild bei Fütterungen unweit des Dorfes beobachten kann. Das Pfeifen der Murmeltiere kann man in einsamen Gebieten häufig hören, zu sehen bekommt man die wachsamen Tiere nur selten. Rehwild lebt von der Talsohle bis zur Waldgrenze und auch der Auer- und der Birkhahn sind im ganzen Tal verbreitet. Die klaren Bäche sind reich an Forellen, so dass auch die Fischer auf ihre Rechnung kommen können. Trotz der starken Rodungstätigkeit ist das Zillertal noch reich an schönen Waldbeständen. Die Hauptholzart ist die Fichte, an der Obergrenze des Waldes ist die Zirbe besonders erwähnenswert. Die Flora ist vielfältig und umfasst die meisten bekannten Alpenblumen, deren Standorte von den Klima- und Bodenverhältnissen abhängen. Wie überall in Tirol sind die seltensten Arten geschützt. Unter besonderem Schutz stehen auch der Scheulingwald bei Mayrhofen, das Lindenwäldchen bei Ramsau und das Linden- und Buchenmischwäldchen, genannt „Glocke" (mit einem Naturerlebnisweg erschlossen) in Finkenberg.

Adlerweg – Wandern auf den Schwingen des Adlers

ADLERWEG

Tirols Hauptwanderweg, der Adlerweg, führt den Wanderer auf seiner Hauptroute quer durch das ganze Land: Von St. Johann im Tiroler Unterland, vorbei am Wilden Kaiser, weiter durch die Brandenberger Alpen, durch das Rofan- und Karwendelgebirge und schließlich durch die Lechtaler Alpen nach St. Anton am Arlberg. Diese Streckenführung ergibt die stilisierte Silhouette eines Adlers. Die Regionalrouten führen in die Seitentäler des Inntals, das Paznaun-, Kauner-, Pitz-, Ötz-, Stubai- und Zillertal, sowie ins Tannheim, in den Kaiserwinkl und in die Kitzbüheler Alpen. Der Jungadler über Osttirol bietet den Wanderern – wie der Adlerweg in Nordtirol – die ganze Vielfalt an Wanderungen in den Bergen: von anspruchsvollen hochalpinen Wanderungen bis hin zu gemütlichen Wanderungen querfeldein reicht das Repertoire. Einheitlich beschildert, gut markiert und detailliert beschrieben führt der Adlerweg durch eine wunderschöne Landschaft hin zu Tirols schönsten Plätzen. Sehen Sie selbst!
Nähere Infos und Tipps unter www.adlerweg.tirol.at

Weitwanderwege

Die OeAV-Sektion Weitwanderer gilt als Auskunftsstelle für alle europäischen Fernwanderwege sowie für die österreichischen Weitwanderwege: Österreichischer Alpenverein, Thaliastraße 159/3/16, 1160 Wien/Österreich, Telefon = Fax (0043) 01/4938408 oder Mobil: 0664/2737242, weitwanderer@sektion.alpenverein.at
www.alpenverein.at/weitwanderer • www.fernwege.de
Durch die alpinen Vereine wurden markierte Wege angelegt, die über große Strecken führen und sowohl mit einer Nummer als auch mit einem Namen bezeichnet sind. Damit sollen Ziele präsentiert werden, die zuvor nur selten besucht wurden, und gleichzeitig auch die Vielfalt der touristischen Möglichkeiten aufgezeigt werden.

Für die Begehung dieser Wege wurde eine eigene Wanderliteratur sog. „Wanderführer" aufgelegt, die dem Begeher den Streckenverlauf, Nächtigungsmöglichkeiten, Entfernungs- und Höhenangaben, Wegzeiten mit Schwierigkeitsgraden sowie Öffnungszeiten von Gasthöfen und Schutzhütten näher bringen. Außerdem wurden Kontrollstellen geschaffen, wo durch einen Stempelabdruck der Besuch dokumentiert wird und danach Wanderabzeichen in verschiedenen Kategorien vergeben, wobei die Zeit, in der die betreffenden Wege zurückgelegt werden, keine Rolle spielt.

In Österreich bestehen neben einer Vielzahl von regionalen Wanderwegen **zehn Weitwanderwege**, die mit den Ziffern 01 bis 10 bezeichnet sind. Eine evtl. vorgesetzte Zahl gibt die Gebirgsgruppen (Hunderterstelle) an. In den Zentralalpen ist diese Grundnummer ungerade (z. B. 702), in den Nördlichen und Südlichen Kalkalpen hingegen gerade (z. B. 801), ein nachfolgender Buchstabe (z. B. 702A) macht darauf aufmerksam, dass es sich um eine Wegvariante handelt. Mehrere nationale Weitwanderwege sind in das internationale Europäische Fernwanderwegenetz mit einbezogen.

Auf dem vorliegenden Kartenblatt scheint der Zentralalpenweg 02 auf.

Bitte erkundigen Sie sich vor Beginn Ihrer Wanderung, ob in den angegebenen Hütten bzw. Orten Übernachtungsmöglichkeiten bestehen. Die Begehung dieser Weitwanderwege erfordert Bergerfahrung, Kondition und eine gute Ausrüstung.

Wegverlauf der Weitwanderwege
Der Zentralalpenweg 02/Hauptweg (502):

Der Zentralalpenweg 02 beginnt in Hainburg an der Donau, reicht bis Feldkirch in Vorarlberg und führt durch alle Bundesländer mit Ausnahme von Oberösterreich und Wien. Er ist der alpinste aller Weitwanderwege und weist eine Länge von ca. 1000 km auf. Da diese Tour großteils durch Hochgebirge – stellenweise Gletscherüberquerung! – führt, sind Bergerfahrung, gute Kondition und die entsprechende Ausrüstung unbedingt erforderlich! In den Talorten stehen auch geprüfte Bergführer zur Verfügung, die Sie sicher bei Ihrer Tour begleiten. Fragen Sie beim Tourismusverband nach. Bitte, erkundigen Sie sich vor Beginn Ihrer Bergtour nach dem aktuellen Zustand der Wege und ob in den angegebenen Hütten Übernachtungsmöglichkeiten bestehen.

Der Weg wird am rechten Kartenrand (K 17), von der Warnsdorfer Hütte kommend, sichtbar, verläuft über die Zillerplattenscharte zur Plauener Hütte. Nun vorbei am Speicher Zillergründl und die Straße talauswärts vorbei an den Gasthöfen „Bärenbad", „In der Au", „Häusling" und „Klaushof" bis in den Bereich von Mayrhofen. Nun geht es die Straße hinein zum Speicher Stillup, und über das Stilluphaus hinauf zur Grüne-Wand-Hütte, um nach steilem Aufstieg die Kasseler Hütte zu erreichen. In großem Bogen vorbei an einigen Dreitausendern, wo sich Kees um Kees reiht, hinauf zur Lapenscharte und absteigend zur Greizerhütte. Weiter verläuft der Weg hinunter in den Floitengrund sowie über Leitern (Trittsicherheit und Schwindelfreiheit erforderlich) steil hinauf in die Mörchenscharte, sowie ebenso steil ins Rosskar und zum Schwarzensee. Schließlich wird die Berliner Hütte erreicht. Nun mühsam, seilgesichert und ausgesetzt über den Schönbichler Grat und weiter auf dem Berliner

8

Höhenweg zum Furtschaglhaus. In Kehren hinunter zum Schlegeisgrund und auf dem Fahrweg den gleichnamigen Speicher entlang bis in den Zamser Grund. Sodann zweigt der Zentralalpenweg in einen Steig ab, der ihn zur Olpererhütte leitet. Steil und mühsam weiter über den Riepengrat zur Alpeiner Scharte und – in äußerste Vorsicht gebietendem Abstieg – zur Geraer Hütte, wo das Kartenblatt (A 7) nach Vals verlassen wird.

Der Zentralalpenweg 02 – Variante (702A, 502A, 302A)

Um schwierige und sehr schwierige Wegteile des Hauptweges zu umgehen, wurden Varianten geschaffen. Auch diese Touren führen großteils durch Hochgebirge – stellenweise Gletscherüberquerung!, es sind daher auch hier Bergerfahrung, gute Kondition und die entsprechende Ausrüstung notwendig! (Siehe Bemerkungen unter Hauptweg).

Beim Zentralalpenweg verläuft in diesem Kartenblatt neben dem Hauptweg eine Variante (702A, 502A, 302A) vom Almdorf Königsleiten, wo die Karte am oberen rechten Rand (K 11) betreten wird, weiter über Gerlos, Gmünd, Hainzenberg und Maria Rast nach Hippach. Entlang der Zillertaler-Höhenstraße bis Grün, wo das Blatt erstmals zur Rastkogelhütte (D 1) verlassen wird, um kurz darauf von der letztgenannten Hütte kommend wieder in die Karte zu treten (C 1). Ein kurzes Stück kann der Weg am oberen Kartenrand über den Rastkogel verfolgt werden, ehe er sich der Weidener Hütte zuwendet (B 1) und abermals das Blatt verlässt. Ein letztes Mal wird das Blatt betreten (A 1), um über das Krovenzjoch zu der auf dem Truppenübungsplatz Lizum-Walchen gelegenen Lizumer Hütte, weiter zum Geier und in den Bereich des Lizumer Reckner zu streben, um kurz darauf das Blatt (A 3) nach Navis zu verlassen.

Höhenwege

Tuxer Alpen

Bei lawinensicheren Verhältnissen Übergänge auch als Skitouren empfehlenswert.

1. Tag:

a) Ausgangspunkt Bergstation der Penkenseilbahn bzw. Gschößwandhaus; von Mayrhofen zu Fuß 3 – 3½ Std.; über den Gschößberg zum Penkenjochhaus (2095 m), 1¼ Std.; weiter zur Wanglalm und über die Wanglspitz (2420 m) und das Hoarbergjoch (2590 m) über Blockwerk zum Gipfel des Rastkogels (2762 m), insgesamt 3½ – 4 Std.

b) Ausgangspunkt Rastkogelhütte, die von Hippach in 4 – 4½ Std. bzw. vom Gasthaus Mösl (Autobushaltestelle) in ca. 1½ – 2 Std. erreicht wird: von der Hütte über die Sidanalm zur Scharte südöstlich des Gipfels und leicht auf den Rastkogel (2762 m), 2 Std.; vom Gipfel über den Westgrat, bzw. etwas südlich davon, zum Nurpensjoch, von dem die Halslspitze (2574 m) leicht erreicht wird und über die Nafingalm zur Weidener Hütte (Nafinghütte, 1856 m), ca. 2 Std.

2. Tag:
Siehe auch Anschlussblatt, KOMPASS-Wanderkarte 37 „Zillertaler Alpen – Tuxer Alpen".
a) Von der Weidener Hütte über das Geiseljoch (2292 m) zur Geiselalm, 2½ Std.; von dort über die Nasse Tuxalm, an den Torseen vorbei zum Torjoch (2386 m), 2½ Std.; Abstieg zur Lizumer Hütte (2019 m), ½ Std., insgesamt 5½ – 6 Std.
b) Von der Weidener Hütte über die Grafennsalm zum Grafensjoch (2450 m) nördlich der Hippoldspitze, 3 Std.; der Gipfel (2642 m) kann von Westen leicht erstiegen werden. Man steigt über den Außerlann-Hochleger und Niederleger ab zur Innerlannalm und von dieser am herrlichen Zirbenweg hinauf zur Lizumer Hütte (2019 m), ca. 2½ Std.

3. Tag:
Von der Lizumer Hütte immer in südlicher Richtung, vorbei am Junssee, führt uns der aussichtsreiche Höhenweg zum Tuxer-Joch-Haus (2310 m), 5 – 6 Std. Fortsetzung der Wanderung entweder nach Westen, siehe Anschlussblatt, KOMPASS-Wanderkarte 36 „Innsbruck – Brenner" oder in 2 Std. Abstieg nach Hintertux.

Zillertaler Alpen
Große West-Ost-Durchquerung, größtenteils auf Alpenvereinswegen (Begehung auch in umgekehrter Richtung möglich).

1. Tag:
Aufstieg zur Geraer Hütte (2326 m); von St. Jodok am Brenner (siehe Anschlussblatt, KOMPASS-Wanderkarte 36 „Innsbruck – Brenner") durch das Valsertal zum Gasthof „Touristenrast", 1½ – 2 Std.; nun dem Alpeiner Bach folgend talein (Ende der Fahrstraße) und in Kehren über die Steilstufe zur Ochsnerhütte (2081 m), hierauf etwas flacher über die Almböden der Alpeiner Alm zum Windschaufelgraben, diesen steil hinauf und in Kehren zur Hütte, insgesamt ca. 4½ Std. – **Variante/1. Tag:** Aufstieg zum Tuxer-Joch-Haus (2310 m): a) Von St. Jodok durch das Schmirntal nach Kasern, ca. 2½ Std.; weiter in den Kaserer Winkl, wo die Fahrstraße endet, ½ Std. und in 2 Std. auf Saumweg zur Hütte, insgesamt ca. 4½ – 5 Std.; b) müheloser von Hintertux, 2½ Std., bei Benützung des Sommerbergalm-Sesselliftes, ¾ Std.

2. Tag:
Von der Hütte links des Alpeiner Ferners (aufgelassenes Bergwerk) empor in die Alpeiner Scharte (2959 m), 2 Std. Dann steigt man jedoch weiter steil in das Unterschrammachkar mit kleinen Seen und in den Zamser Grund ab, durch den man talaus zum Schlegeisspeicher (15-minütige Wanderung zur Dominikushütte, 1805 m, möglich; Bushaltestelle) wandert, 2 – 2½ Std.; nun am Berliner Höhenweg dem Seeufer entlang zum Schlegeisgrund zum Furtschaglboden und in Kehren hinauf zum Furtschaglhaus (2295 m), ca. 2½ Std., insgesamt ca. 7 Std. – **Variante/2. Tag:** Übergang zum Spannagelhaus (2531 m), 2 Std.; nun über die Friesenbergscharte (2910 m) unschwer zum Friesenberghaus (2498 m) am Friesenbergsee, ca. 3½ Std.; von diesem gleich weiter entweder direkt zum Schlegeisspeicher, 1½ Std., oder mit dem Umweg über die Olpererhütte (2388 m), 2 Std., und in einer weiteren guten Stunde zum Stausee absteigen. Hier trifft man auf den Weg zum Furtschaglhaus, siehe oben. Diese Variante kann nur durch Benützung der Liftanlagen von Hintertux verkürzt werden.

3. Tag:
Vom Furtschaglhaus über das aussichtsreiche Schönbichler Horn (3134 m), 2½ – 3 Std.; in östlicher Richtung von der Scharte zunächst steil (Seilsicherung) durch die Flanke auf den Gratrücken und über diesen auf bequemem Plattenweg absteigend zur vollkommen ausgeaperten Zunge des Waxeggkeeses; der Weg überquert die mächtigen Schotterablagerungen am Fuß von Waxegg- und Hornkees und steigt zuletzt kurz zur Berliner Hütte (2042 m) an, insgesamt 5 – 6 Std.

Tuxer-Joch-Haus, 2310 m, und/and/e Gefrorene-Wand-Spitze, 3288 m

4. Tag:
Über den herrlich gelegenen Schwarzensee in das Rosskar (nach links Abzweigung zur Melkerscharte) und in Kehren zur Nördlichen Mörchenscharte (2957 m), 2½ – 3 Std.; jenseits in vielen Kehren (Seilsicherung) über das steile Gelände hinab in den innersten Floitengrund; diesen überquert man und trifft auf der jenseitigen Talseite auf den Hüttenweg, der in etwa ¾ Std. zur Greizerhütte (2227 m) hinaufführt, insgesamt 5½ Std.

5. Tag:
Über die Hänge des Griesfeldes nordwärts, dann in kleinen Kehren in die Lapenscharte (2701 m), 1½ Std.; jenseits unter den Felsen des Gigalitz hinab zu einem Moränenrücken und in das Lapenkar bis zur Wegteilung; rechts führt ein schöner Höhenweg (Seilsicherung) durch die Kare des inneren Stillupgrundes zur Kasseler Hütte (2178 m), insgesamt 4½ – 5 Std.; links steigt man durch das Lapenkar an der Lapenhütte (verfallen) vorbei und zwischen Bächen sehr steil hinab in den Stillupgrund; über eine Brücke führt der Weg zur Taxachalm und zur Grünen-Wand-Hütte (1436 m), insgesamt 4 – 4½ Std.

6. Tag:
Durch den Stillupgrund bis zum Nordende des Speichers, von der Kasseler Hütte ca. 3½ – 4 Std.; von dort über die Krötzelbergalm und die Hahnpfalz auf die Edelhütte (2238 m), 3 – 3½ Std.

7. Tag:
Über die Ahornachalm und Stadelbachalm zum Alpengasthof Häusling (1053 m) im Zillergrund, 4 Std.; talein zum Gasthof „In der Au", 1½ Std. (u. U. Fahrgelegenheit), und weiter in ¾ Std. zum Gasthof Bärenbad. Ein Shuttle-Bus geht bis zum Restaurant Adlerblick. Ausdauernde Geher können noch über das Restaurant Adlerblick und am Dreiländer-Weg dem Speicher Zillergründl entlang zur Plauener Hütte (2364 m) aufsteigen, 2½ Std.; von dieser ist eine Fortsetzung der Tour über die Richterhütte (2367 m) und weiter nach Norden über die Zittauer Hütte nach Gerlos oder nach Osten über das Krimmler Tauernhaus (1631 m) in die Venedigergruppe möglich, siehe Anschlussblatt, KOMPASS-Wanderkarte 38 „Venedigergruppe – Oberpinzgau".

Alpines Notsignal: Sechsmal innerhalb einer Minute in regelmäßigen Zeitabständen ein sichtbares oder hörbares Zeichen geben und hierauf eine Pause von einer Minute eintreten lassen. Das gleiche wird wiederholt, bis Antwort erfolgt.

Antwort: Innerhalb einer Minute wird dreimal in regelmäßigen Zeitabständen ein sichtbares oder hörbares Zeichen gegeben.

DIE ZILLERTAL ACTIVCARD

Die Zillertal Activcard wird im Sommer 2009 wieder für alle geöffneten Zillertaler Seilbahnen (bitte beachten Sie die Öffnungszeiten), die Zillertaler Freischwimmbäder (Fügen, Stumm, Zell, Hippach, Mayrhofen und Finkenberg), die Sternwarte (Planetarium) Königsleiten und die meisten öffentlichen Verkehrsmittel in der Region (Detailinfo siehe Zillertal Activcard-Broschüre) Gültigkeit besitzen (Maut extra!). Ebenfalls erhalten Sie im Sommer 2009 bei Vorlage der Zillertal Activcard wieder mindestens 10% Ermäßigung bei vielen Vorteilspartnern im Zillertal und Umgebung. Die Zillertal Activcard ist bei allen geöffneten Seilbahnstationen, bei den Bahnhöfen Jenbach (nur eingeschränkte Verkaufszeiten), Zell und Mayrhofen, in den Tourismusbüros Fügen, Uderns, Kaltenbach, Zell im Zillertal, Königsleiten, Hippach, Mayrhofen, Tux und bei der Zillertal Tourismus GmbH in Schlitters erhältlich. Die Zillertal Activcard ist nicht übertragbar und nur gültig in Verbindung mit einem Lichtbildausweis (bei Kauf Ausweisvorlage erforderlich) und der Name des Benutzers muss auf der Card vermerkt sein!
Achtung: Mit der Zillertal Activcard ist pro Tag eine Berg- und Talfahrt mit der Seilbahn Ihrer Wahl möglich (Berg- und Talfahrt kann auch bei zwei verschiedenen Bergbahnen erfolgen) und Sie können pro Tag ein Freischwimmbad benützen. Die Zillertal Activcard wird nicht für Paragleiter verkauft! Die Zillertal Activcard ist für 6, 9 oder 12 aufeinanderfolgende Tage erhältlich. Kinderermäßigung: Kinder bis einschließlich Jahrgang 2003 sind frei; Kinder Jahrgänge 1994 – 2002 bezahlen den Kindertarif. Familienkarte: Beim Kauf von zwei Erwachsenenkarten fahren alle Kinder (bis einschließlich Jahrgang 1994) kostenlos – Ausweisvorlage erforderlich.
Informationen: Zillertal Tourismus GmbH, Bundesstraße 27 d, 6262 Schlitters
Tel. 05288/87187 • Fax 87187-1 • www.zillertal.at • info@zillertal.at

Quellenangabe zu Sperrgebieten:
Im Bemühen um eine partnerschaftliche Verträglichkeit von Interessen der Jagd- und Forstwirtschaft mit Bergsteigern, Bikern und Wanderern hat der Österreichische Alpenverein – www.alpenverein.or.at/naturschutz (Bergsport und Umwelt), Telefon + +43/(0)512/ 59547 – eine Datenbank erstellt, in der sämtliche in Österreich vorhandenen jagdlichen, forstlichen und militärischen Sperrgebiete und Wildschutzgebiete sowie alle bedeutenden Natur-, Landschafts- und Sonderschutzgebiete erfasst sind. Die KOMPASS-Karten GmbH dankt dem Österreichischen Alpenverein für die erteilten Informationen zur vorliegenden KOMPASS-Wanderkarte.

Via Alpina Auf 341 Tagesetappen, 5 verschiedenen Routen und über 5000 km Weglänge lädt dieser außergewöhnliche Wanderweg zu einer Entdeckungsreise durch acht Alpenstaaten von Monaco über Frankreich, die Schweiz, Liechtenstein, Deutschland, Österreich, Italien und Slowenien. Der Weg beginnt in Monaco und endet in Triest. Die Via Alpina schlängelt sich zwischen 0 und 3000 Meter Höhe durch den Alpenbogen, durchquert 9 Nationalparks, 17 Naturparks, zahlreiche Naturschutzgebiete und überschreitet 60 mal die Staatsgrenzen. Die Routen weisen keine technischen Schwierigkeiten auf, sind also in den Sommermonaten mit einer angemessenen Wanderausrüstung ohne Seil und Steigeisen zu begehen. Jede Etappe verfügt über ein oder mehrere Übernachtungsmöglichkeiten in Tallagen oder auf den Schutzhütten der alpinen Vereine.

Als ein Projekt der 1991 von den Alpenstaaten unterzeichneten Alpenkonvention steht für die Via Alpina die Förderung einer nachhaltigen Entwicklung und das Bewusstsein für die Schutzwürdigkeit des sensiblen Lebensraumes Alpen im Vordergrund. Schließlich sind die Alpen nicht nur der größte europäische Naturraum und ein Rückzugsgebiet für eine einzigartige Flora und Fauna, sondern auch Heimat von ca. 13 Millionen Menschen, geprägt von uralten Traditionen und kulturellem Austausch. Weitere Informationen finden Sie unter www.via-alpina.org

Alpine Notrufnummern

Europaweit: 112 • Italien: 118 • Österreich: 140

Alpengasthöfe und Unterkunftshütten

Alle Angaben ohne Gewähr! Bitte erfragen Sie vor Beginn der Wanderung im Talort die Bewirtschaftungszeit und erkundigen Sie sich, ob eine Übernachtungsmöglichkeit besteht!
Die Telefonnummern der wichtigsten Alpengasthöfe und Unterkunftshütten finden Sie auf Seite 76.

Tuxer Alpen

Astegg, 1176 m (D 2), privater Gasthof, Postleitzahl: 6292 Finkenberg, ganzjährig bewirtschaftet. Zugänge: von Finkenberg, 1 Std.; von Mayrhofen, 2 Std. Übergänge: zum Penkenhaus, 1½ Std.; zum Gschößwandhaus, 2 Std.

Bergrast, 1794 m (D 2), Gasthof am Gschößberg, siehe Gschößwandhaus.

Eggalm, 1948 m (B 3), privates Restaurant, Postleitzahl: 6293 Lanersbach, ganzjährig bewirtschaftet. Zugänge: von Lanersbach, 2¼ Std. oder mit der Gondelbahn. Übergang: zur Lizumer Hütte, 4 Std. Gipfel: Grüblspitze, 2395 m, 1 Std. (leicht).

Gschößwandhaus, 1762 m (D 2), Bergstation der Penkenbahn, privat, Postleitzahl: 6290 Mayrhofen, ganzjährig bewirtschaftet. Zugänge: von Finkenberg, ca. 3 Std.; von Mayrhofen, 3 – 3½ Std. Übergänge: zum Penkenjochhaus über den Gschößberg, 1¼ Std.; zum Penkenhaus, 1¼ Std.; zum Mösl-Gasthaus, 1½ Std. Gipfel: Gschößberg, 2005 m, ½ Std. (leicht).

Lizumer Hütte, 2019 m (A 2), Alpenverein, Postleitzahl: 6112 Wattens, im Winter und Sommer bewirtschaftet. Zugänge: von Wattens, 5 Std.; von Walchen (bis dorthin mit dem Auto), 2 Std. Übergänge: nach Lanersbach, 3½ Std.; zur Weidener Hütte über die Krovenzjoch, 5 Std.; zum Tuxer-Joch-Haus, 6 Std. Gipfel: Mölser Sonnenspitze, 2427 m, 2 Std. (leicht); Geier, 2857 m, 3 Std. (leicht); Lizumer Reckner, 2886 m, 3½ Std. (nur für Geübte).

Penkenhaus, 1814 m (D 2), privat, Postleitzahl: 6292 Finkenberg, ganzjährig bewirtschaftet. Zugänge: von Mayrhofen, 3¾ Std.; von Finkenberg über Astegg, 2½ – 3 Std.; von der Bergstation der Penkenbahn, 1¼ Std. Übergang: zum Penkenjochhaus, ¾ Std.

Penkenjochhaus, 2095 m (D 2), privat, Postleitzahl: 6292 Finkenberg, ganzjährig bewirtschaftet. Zugänge: von Finkenberg über das Penkenhaus, 3½ Std.; von Mayrhofen, 4 – 4½ Std.; von der Bergstation der Penkenbahn, 1¼ Std. Übergang: über die Schrofenalm nach Vorderlanersbach, 2½ Std.; zur Rastkogelhütte über den Rastkogel, ca. 4 Std. Gipfel: Wanglspitz, 2420 m, 1½ Std. (leicht); Rastkogel, 2762 m, 3 Std. (leicht).

Perler, 1130 m (D 1), privater Alpengasthof, Postleitzahl: 6283 Hippach, ganzjährig bewirtschaftet. Zugänge: von Hippach, 1½ Std., auch mit dem Auto erreichbar. Übergang: zur Rastkogelhütte, 3 Std.

13

Zillertaler Alpen
(Tuxer Hauptkamm, Zillertaler Hauptkamm und Reichenspitzgruppe)

Adlerblick, 1900 m (I 16), privates Restaurant, Postleitzahl: 6290 Mayrhofen, im Sommer bewirtschaftet. Zugang: mit dem Auto oder Autobus bis Bärenbad; dann entweder zu Fuß in 45 Min. oder mit dem Shuttle-Bus. In der Nähe die neue Hochgebirgskapelle.

Alpenrose, 1398 m (E 3, F 15), privater Gasthof, Postleitzahl: 6290 Mayrhofen, im Sommer bewirtschaftet. Zugang: von Mayrhofen, 2 – 2 ½ Std. Übergang: zur Edelhütte, 2 ½ Std.

Alpenrosehütte, 1873 m (D 8), privat, Postleitzahl: 6295 Ginzling, im Sommer bewirtschaftet. Zugänge: von Ginzling, 4 ½ Std.; vom Gasthaus Breitlahner, Bushaltestelle, 2 ½ Std. Übergänge: zur Berliner Hütte, ½ Std.; zum Furtschaglhaus, 5 ½ – 6 Std.

Bärenbad, 1450 m (I 16), privat, Postleitzahl: 6290 Mayrhofen, im Sommer bewirtschaftet. Zugänge: von Mayrhofen, 4 ½ Std.; auch mit dem Auto (Mautstraße – Kontingent) bzw. Autobus erreichbar. Übergang: zur Plauener Hütte, 2 Std.

Berliner Hütte, 2042 m (D 8), Alpenverein, Postleitzahl: 6295 Ginzling, im Sommer bewirtschaftet. Zugänge: von Ginzling, 4 ½ Std.; vom Gasthaus Breitlahner, Bushaltestelle, ca. 3 Std. Übergänge: zur Alpenrosehütte, 20 Minuten; zur Greizerhütte über die Nördliche Mörchenscharte, ca. 5 ½ – 6 Std.; zum Furtschaglhaus über das Schönbichler Horn, ca. 6 Std.; in die Gunggl über die Melkerscharte, 6 – 7 Std. Gipfel: Schönbichler Horn, 3134 m, 4 Std. Zahlreiche hochalpine Touren verschiedener Schwierigkeitsgrade.

Brandberger Kolmhaus, 1845 m (G 14), privat, Postleitzahl: 6290 Mayrhofen, im Sommer bewirtschaftet. Zugänge: von Brandberg, ca. 2 Std.; von Mayrhofen, 3 ½ – 4 Std. Übergänge: in das Gerlostal zum Gasthof Kühle Rast (Bushaltestelle) über das Brandberger Joch, 3 ½ Std.; zum Berghotel Gerlosstein, 2 ½ Std. Gipfel: Brandberger Kolm, 2700 m, 2 ½ – 3 Std. (mittel); Torhelm, 2452 m, 2 Std. (leicht).

Breitlahner, 1256 m (C 6), privates Gasthaus, Postleitzahl: 6295 Ginzling, im Sommer bewirtschaftet. Zugänge: von Ginzling, 2 Std.; mit dem Auto bzw. Autobus bis zum Haus. Übergänge: zur Berliner Hütte, 3 Std.; zur Dominikushütte, 2 Std.; zum Friesenberghaus, 4 Std.

Dominikushütte, 1805 m (B 7), privat, Postleitzahl: 6295 Ginzling, im Sommer bewirtschaftet. Zugänge: mit dem Auto (Mautstraße) oder Autobus erreichbar; von Ginzling, 4 ½ Std.; vom Gasthaus Breitlahner, 2 Std. Übergänge: zum Pfitscher-Joch-Haus (Südtirol), 2 Std.; zum Friesenberghaus, 2 ½ Std.; zur Olpererhütte, 2 Std.; zum Furtschaglhaus, 2 ½ Std. Gipfel: Olperer, 3476 m, 5 Std. (nur für Geübte).

Edelhütte, 2238 m (E 4, F 16), Alpenverein, Postleitzahl: 6290 Mayrhofen, im Sommer bewirtschaftet. Zugänge: von Mayrhofen, 4 ½ – 5 Std.; von der Bergstation der Ahornbahn, 1 Std. Übergänge: in den Stilluppgrund zum Stilluphaus, 2 ½ Std. Gipfel: Ahornspitze, 2973 m, 2 – 2 ½ Std. (nur für Geübte).

Finkau, 1420 m (K 13), privates Gasthaus, Postleitzahl: 5743 Krimml, ganzjährig bewirtschaftet. Zugänge: mit dem Auto bis zum Haus oder zu Fuß vom Gerlospass, 2 Std.; von Gerlos, 3 Std. Übergang: zur Zittauer Hütte, 3 Std.

Friesenbergsee mit/with/con Hochfeiler, 3509 m und/and/e Hochferner, 3470 m

Friesenberghaus, 2498 m (B 6), Alpenverein, Postleitzahl: 6295 Ginzling, im Sommer bewirtschaftet. Zugänge: vom Gasthaus Breitlahner, 3½ Std.; von der Dominikushütte, 2 Std. Übergänge: zum Spannagelhaus über die Friesenbergscharte, 3 Std.; zur Olpererhütte, 2 Std. Gipfel: Hoher Riffler, 3231 m, 2 Std., nur Wegspuren (nur für Geübte); Petersköpfl, 2679 m, ¾ Std. (leicht).

Furtschaglhaus, 2295 m (C 9), Alpenverein, Postleitzahl: 6295 Ginzling, im Sommer bewirtschaftet. Zugang: von der Dominikushütte, 2½ Std. Übergang: zur Berliner Hütte über das Schönbichler Horn, 6½ Std. Gipfel: Schönbichler Horn, 3134 m, 2½ Std. (mittel). Zahlreiche Hochgebirgstouren verschiedener Schwierigkeitsgrade.

Gamshütte, 1921 m (D 4), Alpenverein, Postleitzahl: 6290 Mayrhofen, im Sommer bewirtschaftet. Zugänge: von Finkenberg, 3 Std.; von Ginzling, 3 Std. Gipfel: Grinbergspitzen, 2884 m, 2765 bzw. 2867 m, ca. 2½ Std. (mittel).

Geraer Hütte, 2324 m (A 7), Alpenverein, Postleitzahl: 6154 St. Jodok am Brenner, im Sommer bewirtschaftet. Zugänge: von St. Jodok, 4½ Std.; mit dem Auto bzw. Autobus bis zum Gasthaus Touristenrast, von dort 2½ Std. Übergänge: zur Olpererhütte, 4 Std.; nach Schmirn am Wildlahnerweg, 2½ Std.; zum Tuxer-Joch-Haus über die Kleegrubenscharte, 4 – 4½ Std.

Gerlosstein-Berghotel, 1620 m (G 13), privater Gasthof, Postleitzahl: 6280 Hainzenberg, ganzjährig bewirtschaftet. Zugänge: nahe der Bergstation der Gerlossteinbahn; von Hainzenberg, Autobushaltestelle Ötschenwirt, 2 Std.; von Zell am Ziller, 3½ Std.; von Ramsberg, 2½ – 3 Std. Übergänge: nach Mayrhofen, 3 Std.; zum Brandberger Kolmhaus, 2½ – 3 Std. Gipfel: Gerlossteinwand, 2166 m, 1½ Std. (leicht); Hochfeld, 2350 m, 2 Std. (leicht).

Grawandhütte, 1636 m (C 8), privat, Postleitzahl: 6295 Ginzling, im Sommer bewirtschaftet. Zugang: vom Gasthaus Breitlahner, 1½ Std. Übergang: zur Alpenrosehütte, ¾ Std.

Greizerhütte, 2227 m (E 7, F 19), Alpenverein, Postleitzahl: 6290 Mayrhofen, im Sommer bewirtschaftet. Zugang: von Ginzling, 4 Std. Übergänge: zur Berliner Hütte über die Nördliche Mörchenscharte, 5½ Std.; zur Grüne-Wand-Hütte über die Lapenscharte, 4 Std.; zur Kasseler Hütte, 5 Std. Gipfel: Großer Löffler, 3378 m, 3½ Std. (mittel); Schwarzenstein, 3369 m, 4 Std. (mittel).

Grüne-Wand-Hütte, 1436 m (G 18), privat, Postleitzahl: 6290 Mayrhofen, im Sommer bewirtschaftet. Zugänge: von Mayrhofen, 4 Std. oder Taxi ab dem Europahaus in Mayrhofen; vom Alpengasthof Wasserfall, 2 Std. Übergänge: zur Kasseler Hütte, 2 Std.; zur Greizerhütte über die Lapenscharte, 6 Std.

Häusling, 1053 m (GH 15), privater Alpengasthof, Postleitzahl: 6290 Mayrhofen, ganzjährig bewirtschaftet. Zugänge: von Mayrhofen, 2½ Std.; auch mit dem Auto (Mautstraße – Kontingent) bzw. Autobus erreichbar. Übergang: zum Gasthof In der Au, 1½ Std.; auch mit dem Auto oder Autobus erreichbar.

Hochferner-Biwak (Günther-Messner-Biwak), 2429 m (B 9), Alpenverein, ganzjährig zugänglich. Zugänge: von St. Jakob in Pfitsch, 4 Std.; von Stein, 3 Std.; von der 5. Kurve der Pfitscher-Joch-Straße, 1 Std.

Höllensteinhütte, 1710 m (B 4), privat, Postleitzahl: 6293 Lanersbach, im Sommer bewirtschaftet. Zugang: von der Autobushaltestelle Juns (ca. 2 km südlich von Lanersbach), 1½ Std.

In der Au, 1265 m (H 16), privater Gasthof, Postleitzahl: 6290 Mayrhofen, ganzjährig bewirtschaftet. Zugänge: von Mayrhofen, 4 Std.; auch mit dem Auto (Mautstraße – Kontingent) bzw. Autobus erreichbar. Übergang: nach Bärenbad, ¾ Std.

Innerböden, 1301 m (D 5), privater Gasthof, Postleitzahl: 6295 Ginzling, ganzjährig bewirtschaftet. Zugang: von Ginzling, 1 Std.

Kasseler Hütte, 2178 m (G 18), Alpenverein, Postleitzahl: 6290 Mayrhofen, im Sommer bewirtschaftet. Zugänge: von Mayrhofen, ca. 6 Std.; von der Grünen-Wand-Hütte, 2 Std. (bis dorthin Taxi ab dem Europahaus in Mayrhofen). Übergang: Höhenweg über die Lapenscharte zur Greizerhütte, 4 – 5 Std.; zur Edelhütte auf dem Siebenschneidensteig, 9 – 10 Std. Gipfel: Grüne-Wand-Spitze, 2946 m, 2½ Std.; Wollbachspitze, 3209 m, 3 Std.

Klaushof, 1022 m (G 15), privater Gasthof, Postleitzahl: 6290 Mayrhofen, ganzjährig bewirtschaftet. Zugang: von Mayrhofen, 2 Std.; auch mit dem Auto (Mautstraße – Kontingent) bzw. Autobus erreichbar. Übergang: nach Häusling, ½ Std.

Lacknerbrunn, 1006 m (D 3), privater Alpengasthof, Postleitzahl: 6290 Mayrhofen, ganzjährig bewirtschaftet. Zugänge: von Mayrhofen, 1½ Std.; mit dem Auto (Mautstraße) oder Taxi ab dem Europahaus in Mayrhofen. Übergänge: zum Alpengasthof Wasserfall, ¾ Std.; zur Edelhütte, 4 Std.

Max-Hütte, 1445 m (D 6), privat, Postleitzahl: 6292 Finkenberg, im Sommer bewirtschaftet. Zugang: von Ginzling, 1½ Std. Übergang: zur Berliner Hütte über die Melkerscharte, 7 Std.

Olpererhütte, 2388 m (B 7), Alpenverein, Postleitzahl: 6295 Ginzling, im Sommer bewirtschaftet. Zugang: vom Schlegeisspeicher (bis dorthin mit dem Auto/Mautstraße oder Autobus), 1½ Std. Übergänge: zum Friesenberghaus, 2 Std.; zur Geraer Hütte über die Alpeiner Scharte, 4 Std. Gipfel: Olperer, 3476 m, 3 Std. (nur für Geübte); Gefrorene-Wand-Spitzen, 3288 m, 3½ Std. (nur für Geübte).

Pfitscher-Joch-Haus (Rif. Passo di Vizze), 2275 m (A 9), privat, Postleitzahl: 39040 St. Jakob in Pfitsch, im Sommer bewirtschaftet. Zugänge: von Stein, 1¼ Std.; von St. Jakob, 1¾ Std.; vom Schlegeisspeicher, 2 Std. Übergänge: zur Landshuter Europahütte, 3½ Std.; zur Geraer Hütte, 5 Std.; zum Furtschaglhaus, 5 Std. Gipfel: Schrammacher, 3410 m, 4 Std. (nur für Geübte); Hohe Wand-Spitze, 3289 m, 4 Std. (schwierig).

Plauener Hütte, 2364 m (K 16), Alpenverein, Postleitzahl: 6283 Hippach, im Sommer bewirtschaftet. Zugänge: von Mayrhofen, 7½ – 8 Std.; mit dem Auto (Mautstraße – Kontingent) bzw. Autobus bis Bärenbad, von dort 2 Std. Übergang: zur Richterhütte über die Gamsscharte, 3 Std. Gipfel: Richterspitze, 3052 m, 2½ Std. (mittel).

Richterhütte, 2367 m (K 16), Alpenverein, Postleitzahl: 5743 Krimml, im Sommer bewirtschaftet. Zugänge: vom Krimmler Tauernhaus, 2½ Std.; von Krimml, 5 – 6 Std. Übergänge: zur Plauener Hütte, 3 Std.; zur Zittauer Hütte, 3½ Std.; zur Birnlückenhütte, 7¼ Std. Gipfel: Windbachtalkogel, 2843 m, 1½ Std. (leicht); Richterspitze, 3052 m, 2½ Std. (mittel).

Rosshag, 1096 m (C 6), privater Gasthof, Postleitzahl: 6295 Ginzling, ganzjährig bewirtschaftet. Zugänge: von Ginzling, 1 Std. oder mit dem Auto. Übergang: zum Gasthaus Breitlahner, 1 Std. oder mit dem Auto.

Schwarzensteinhütte (Rifugio Vittorio Veneto), 2922 m (E 8), CAI, Post I-39030 Luttach, im Sommer bewirtschaftet. Zugang: von Luttach, 5½ Std. Gipfel: Schwarzenstein, 3369 m, 1½ Std. (mittel).

Spannagelhaus, 2531 m (A 6), Österreichischer Touristenclub, Postleitzahl: 6294 Hintertux, im Sommer und Winter bewirtschaftet. Wenige Minuten neben der Hütte liegt die Spannagelhöhle! Zugänge: von Hintertux, 3½ Std. oder mit der Seilbahn. Übergänge: zum Tuxer-Joch-Haus, 1½ Std.; zum Friesenberghaus über die Friesenbergscharte, 3½ Std. In der Nähe der Hütte befindet sich ein Klettergarten. Erfahrene Bergführer lehren Sie die Grundbegriffe des Bergsteigens wie Trittsicherheit, Seiltechnik, richtiges Klettern usw.

Wanderer: im Hintergrund die Reichenspitzgruppe/Hikers: Reichenspitz Group in the background/Escursionisti: sullo sfondo il gruppo della Reichenspitze

16

Stein, 1555 m (A 10), privater Gasthof, Postleitzahl: 39040 St. Jakob in Pfitsch, ganzjährig bewirtschaftet. Zugänge: von St. Jakob in Pfitsch, 1 Std.; auch mit dem Auto erreichbar. Übergang: zur Landshuter Europahütte über das Pfitscher Joch, 4 ¾ Std.

Steinerkogl, 1270 m (E 2, F 14), privates Berggasthaus, Postleitzahl: 6290 Mayrhofen, ganzjährig bewirtschaftet. Zugänge: von Mayrhofen, 1½ Std.; von Brandberg, ¾ Std. Übergänge: zum Brandberger Kolmhaus, 2 Std.; zum Gerlosstein-Berghotel, 2½ Std.

Stilluphaus, 1192 m (FG 17), privat, Postleitzahl: 6290 Mayrhofen, im Sommer bewirtschaftet. Zugänge: von Mayrhofen, 3 Std. oder Taxi ab dem Europahaus in Mayrhofen; vom Alpengasthof Wasserfall, 1 Std. Übergang: zur Grüne-Wand-Hütte, 1 Std.

Tuxer-Joch-Haus, 2310 m (A 5), Österreichischer Touristenklub, Postleitzahl: 6294 Hintertux, im Sommer bewirtschaftet. Zugänge: von Hintertux, 2½ Std.; von der Bergstation bei der Sommerbergalm, ¾ Std.; von Kasern im Schmirntal, 2 Std. Übergänge: zum Spannagelhaus, 2 Std.; zur Geraer Hütte über die Kleegrubenscharte, 4½ Std. Gipfel: Hornspitze, 2650 m, 1½ Std. (nur für Geübte); Frauenwand, 2541 m, 1 Std. (leicht).

Wasserfall, 1120 m (E 4, F 16), privater Alpengasthof im Stillupgrund, Postleitzahl: 6290 Mayrhofen, im Sommer bewirtschaftet. Zugänge: von Mayrhofen, 2 Std.; mit dem Auto (Mautstraße) oder Taxi ab dem Europahaus in Mayrhofen erreichbar. Übergang: über das Stilluphaus zur Grüne-Wand-Hütte, 2 Std.

Wiesenhof, 1058 m (E 3, F 15), privater Gasthof, Postleitzahl: 6290 Mayrhofen, ganzjährig bewirtschaftet. Zugänge: von Mayrhofen, 1½ Std. oder Zufahrt mit dem Auto möglich.

Zittauer Hütte, 2328 m (K 14), Alpenverein, Postleitzahl: 5743 Krimml, im Sommer bewirtschaftet. Zugänge: vom Gasthaus Finkau, 3 Std.; von Gerlos, 5 Std.; vom Gerlospass, 5 Std. Übergänge: zum Krimmler Tauernhaus, 3 Std.; zur Richterhütte, 3½ Std. Gipfel: Rosskopf, 2845 m, 1½ Std. (leicht); Reichenspitze, 3303 m, 4 Std. (schwierig).

Naturpark Zillertaler Alpen

Seit 1991 steht die Nordtiroler Seite des Alpenhauptkamms vom Olperer bis zur Salzburger Landesgrenze auf einer Fläche von 372 km² unter Schutz. Der Naturpark liegt auf dem Gebiet der Gemeinden Brandberg, Finkenberg, Mayrhofen sowie der Fraktion Ginzling und seine Einrichtung konnte nur durch die gute Zusammenarbeit des Österreichischen Alpenvereins (ÖAV), der Gemeinden sowie der Abteilung Umweltschutz des Landes Tirol erreicht werden. Der Reiz dieser einzigartigen Natur- und Kulturlandschaft im hinteren Zillertal soll erhalten und vor harten Erschließungen bewahrt werden, wie etwa: Straßen für den öffentlichen Verkehr, Seilbahnen und Liftinfrastruktur zur Personenbeförderung, Lärm erregende Betriebe, Hubschrauberflüge zu touristischen Zwecken.

Der Wanderer erlebt in den Seitentälern Zillgrund, Stillupgrund, Floitengrund, Gunggl, Zemmgrund und Zamser Grund Natur pur. Zwischen Naturschutz und Tourismus ist in den letzten Jahren ein neuer Weg entstanden, seit 2002 sind auch die Tourismusverbände in den Naturpark eingebunden. Der Wanderer erlebt in der Naturparkregion „das andere Zillertal", egal ob bei einem leichten Spaziergang oder auf einer mehrtägigen Hüttentour. Im Naturpark liegen acht Alpenvereinshütten – die Berliner Hütte wurde alpenweit als erste unter Denkmalschutz gestellt – und ein dichtes Netz von hervorragend gepflegten Wanderwegen. Damit das Schutzgebiet der Verordnung nicht sich selbst überlassen bleibt, hat der ÖAV ein Projekt mit Modellcharakter gestartet. Es wurde eine hauptamtliche Schutzgebietsbetreuung eingerichtet, das Büro der Naturparkbetreuung ist derzeit im Alpenvereinsheim in Mayrhofen untergebracht. Die tragenden Säulen der als Verein organisierten Betreuung sind das Land Tirol, der ÖAV, die vier genannten Gemeinden sowie die Tourismusverbände Mayrhofen-Hippach und Tux-Finkenberg.

Der Naturpark Zillertaler Alpen (Nordtirol) bildet zusammen mit dem Naturpark Rieserferner – Ahrn (Südtirol) sowie dem Nationalpark Hohe Tauern grenzüberschreitend auf ca. 2.500 km² den größten Schutzgebietsverbund der Alpen. Entdecken Sie die Naturparkregion Zillertaler Alpen und seine Schutzgebietsnachbarn! Sehr gute Möglichkeiten dazu bieten das Naturpark-Sommerprogramm mit geführten Themenwanderungen sowie die Naturpark-Ausstellungen im Bergsteigerdorf Ginzling!

Informationsstelle: Naturpark Zillertaler Alpen, Sportplatzstraße 307, 6290 Mayrhofen
Telefon = Fax: 0043/(0)5285/63601
naturpark.zillertal@alpenverein.at • www.naturpark-zillertal.at

Wir danken den Tourismusverbänden und alpinen Vereinen, die uns bei der Aktualisierung des vorliegenden KOMPASS-Lexikons tatkräftig unterstützt und uns Bildmaterial zur Verfügung gestellt haben.

Ortsbeschreibungen

Die Telefon- und Faxnummern der Tourismusverbände bzw. Gemeindeämter finden Sie auf Seite 77.

BRANDBERG   E 2/F 14

Gemeinde, Bezirk Schwaz, Einwohner: 350, Höhe: 1082 m, Postleitzahl: 6290. **Auskunft:** Gemeindeamt Brandberg. **Bahnstation:** Mayrhofen (6 km). **Busverbindung:** mit Mayrhofen.

Hoch über dem Zillergrund liegt auf steiler Berglehne das kleine Erholungsdorf Brandberg. Erst Anfang des 19. Jahrhunderts wurde von der alten „Hauptmannschaft (= Gemeinde) Pramberg" Mayrhofen als selbständige Gemeinde abgetrennt. Dadurch wurde Brandberg mit seinen Weilern, Einzelhöfen, Asten und Almen am sonnigen Hang des „Pram-" oder „Brandberges" und im langgestreckten Zillergrund eine echte Bergbauerngemeinde. In letzter Zeit entwickelte es sich zu einer beliebten Tourismusgemeinde.

Brandberg, mit 156 km² eine der flächenmäßig größten Gemeinden des Zillertales, ist klimatisch gut gelegen und ideal für zahlreiche Wanderungen. Ur- und Kulturlandschaft bieten dem Naturliebhaber ein großes Erlebnisangebot. In den Ort führt eine gut ausgebaute Zufahrtsstraße; im Ort gibt es genügend Parkplätze.

Sehenswert im Ort und in der Umgebung

In der klassizistischen **Pfarrkirche zum hl. Kreuz** ist am Seitenaltar eine spätgotische Madonna sehenswert; an der Außenseite ein Kriegerdenkmal; über dem Portal die „Mater dolorosa"; Mosaikarbeiten; neue Friedhofskapelle von 1977/78. – **Dorfbrunnen** mit Kleinplastik des Bildschnitzers Albin Moroder aus Mayrhofen. – Von diesem stammen auch die **Kreuzwegtafeln** am Weg zur Brandberger Kapelle. – **Naturpark Zillertaler Alpen**.

Spazierwege und Bergtouren

Zum Berggasthaus Steinerkogl (1270 m) über Emberg, ¾ Std. – Zum Brandberger Kolmhaus (1845 m), ca. 2 Std. und weiter zum Brandberger Kolm (2700 m), insgesamt ca. 4½ Std. – Zum Gerlosstein-Berghotel (1620 m), über die Laberg- und Kotahornalm, 3½ Std. – In den Zillergrund bis zum Gasthaus Klaushof (1022 m), ca. 1 Std., weiter bis zum Gasthof Häusling, insgesamt ca. 1½ Std., weiter bis zum Gasthaus In der Au (1265 m), insgesamt 3 Std., weiter bis zum Gasthaus Bärenbad (1450 m), insgesamt 4 Std. Diese Strecke kann auch mit dem eigenen Auto auf der Mautstraße (Kontingent!) oder mit dem Autobus zurückgelegt werden. – Von Bärenbad bis zum Speicher Zillergründl, ca. 1½ Std. – Zur Plauener Hütte (2364 m), ab Bärenbad, 2 Std. – Zum Restaurant Adlerblick (1900 m), 45 Min. ab Bärenbad oder mit dem Shuttle-Bus. – Zur Kainzenhüttenalm (1550 m) im Sundergrund, ab In der Au, ca. 1½ Std. – Auf die Bodenalm (1670 m), ab Häusling, ca. 1½ Std.

FINKENBERG   D 3

Gemeinde, Bezirk Schwaz, Einwohner: 1520, Höhe: 839 m, Postleitzahl: 6292. **Auskunft:** Tourismusverband Tux – Finkenberg. **Bahnstation:** Mayrhofen (3 km). **Busverbindung:** mit Mayrhofen und bis zur Talstation der Hintertuxer Gletscherbahnen in Hintertux. **Bergbahnen:** Finkenberger Almbahnen, mehrere Sessel- und Schlepplifte im Bereich des Penkenjoches.

Der im Sommer und Winter beliebte Tourismusort liegt auf einer sonnigen Terrasse hoch über der tief eingeschnittenen Mündungsklamm des Tuxbaches. Finkenberg ist flächenmäßig die zweitgrößte Gemeinde des Zillertales, allerdings entfällt mehr als die Hälfte ihres Gebietes auf Ödland. Zu ihr gehören nicht nur die zum Teil schon Anfang des 14. Jahrhunderts urkundlich erwähnten Höfe und Weiler, die auf der Sonnenseite des äußeren Tuxer Tales bis ungefähr 1400 m ansteigen sowie die darüber liegenden Asten und Almen, sondern

18

sie greift am westlichen Ufer des Zemmbaches entlang bis in den Talschluss des Zamser und Schlegeisgrundes und an die heutige Staatsgrenze nach Süden.

Im Jahr 1991 wurde diese unverwechselbare Gebirgslandschaft als „Ruhegebiet Zillertaler Hauptkamm" (nun Naturpark Zillertaler Alpen), durch die Tiroler Landesregierung unter Schutz gestellt. Das bedeutet, dass hier in Zukunft keine Schilifte und keine öffentlich befahrbaren Straßen errichtet werden dürfen.

Finkenberg wurde im Winter 1980 weltbekannt, als Leonhard Stock durch seinen Abfahrts-Olympiasieg die Goldmedaille errang und damit auch den Weltmeistertitel.

Sehenswert im Ort und in der Umgebung

Die **Pfarrkirche zum hl. Leonhard**, erbaut 1720, im 19. Jahrhundert erweitert; Innenausstattung großteils aus der Bauzeit. – Die **Teufelsbrücke** über die tief eingeschnittene Klamm des Tuxbaches ist eine Holzkonstruktion aus dem Jahr 1876. – Kleiner **Wasserfall** oberhalb des Dorfes. – **Naturerlebnisweg Glocke.** – **Moorlehrpfad am Penkenjoch.**

Spazierwege und Bergtouren

Von der Kirche über Sporer – Wasserfall – Waldweg und zurück, 1 Std. – Nach Stein (Gasthof Gletscherblick), Aufstieg von der Kirche und Abstieg über Persal zur Teufelsbrücke, von dort am Klammweg zurück, 2 Std. – Rundgang von der Kirche über die Teufelsbrücke zum Gasthof Schöne Aussicht, weiter am Ausgleichsbecken Dornau vorüber am Martins Wirtshaus zum Jochberg, auf der Straße über die Pension Forellenhof zur Pension Hochsteg, von dort am Rande der Klamm zurück zur Teufelsbrücke und über diese ins Dorf, insgesamt ca. 2½ Std. – Zum Gasthof Astegg (1176 m) über Stein, 1 Std.; Abstieg gegen Mayrhofen am Mariensteig, von dem man westlich des Zemmbaches auf der Wiesenweg, der nach Finkenberg zurückführt, abzweigt, ca. 2 Std. – Nach Innerberg (Autobushaltestelle) auf der Straße über Persal, ¾ Std.; über die Rosengartenbrücke nach Gschwendt und Brunnhaus und zurück über die Teufelsbrücke oder über den Steg und am Schwimmbad vorbei zur Straße bei Persal, 2½ – 3 Std. – Nach Vorderlanersbach über Altenstall – Katzenmoos – Möser – Außerrettenbach, 3 Std. – Zum Gschößwandhaus (1762 m) über den Gasthof Astegg, 3 Std. – Zum Penkenhaus (1814 m), 3 Std.; weiter zum Penkenjochhaus (2095 m), Bergstation der Finkenberger Almbahn, ¾ Std. – Zur Gamshütte (1921 m) über den Hermann-Hecht-Weg, 3 Std. – Zum Gasthaus Innerböden (1301 m) und zur Oberbödenalm (1500 m), von Ginzling, 2 Std. – Zur Max-Hütte (1445 m), von Ginzling, 1½ Std. – Zur Greizerhütte (2227 m), von Ginzling durch den Floitengrund, ca. 3¼ Std. – Zum Gasthaus Breitlahner (1256 m), von Ginzling, 1½ Std. – Zur Berliner Hütte (2042 m), ab dem Gasthaus Breitlahner durch den Zemmgrund, über die Grawand- und Alpenrosehütte, 2½ Std. – Zur Dominikushütte (1805 m), von Ginzling, 4½ Std. – Zum Furtschaglhaus (2295 m), von der Dominikushütte aus über das Zamsgatterl und auf dem Berliner Höhenweg, dem Schlegeisspeicher entlang, zur Hütte, 3 Std. – Zum Pfitscher-Joch-Haus (2275 m) von der Dominikushütte aus über das Zamsgatterl und im Zamser Grund zum Pfitscher Joch und zur Hütte, 2 Std. – Zur Olpererhütte (2388 m) von der Dominikushütte zuerst ca. 10 Min. entlang des Stausees, bis zur Abzweigung (Weg 502) nach rechts zur Hütte, 1 Std. – Zum Friesenberghaus (2498 m) zuerst zur Olpererhütte und von dort auf dem Berliner Höhenweg (Weg 526) am Friesenbergsee vorbei zur Hütte, 3 Std. oder direkt vom Stausee zur Hütte (Weg 532), 2 Std.

GERLOS I 12

Gemeinde, Bezirk Schwaz, Einwohner: 800, Höhe: 1245 m, Postleitzahl: 6281. **Auskunft:** Tourismusverband Gerlos – Zell. **Bahnstation:** Zell am Ziller (18 km). **Busverbindung:** mit Zell am Ziller, Mayrhofen und Wald im Pinzgau. **Bergbahnen:** Mehrere Sessel- und Schlepplifte.

Mit dem Ausbau der Bundesstraße über den Gerlospass, 1531 m, dem Bau des Speichers Durlaßboden, der Errichtung von Schigebieten und der Schaffung moderner Tourismusein-

richtungen hielt das technische Zeitalter nun auch in dem bislang recht abgeschiedenen Gerlostal Einzug. Doch gleich abseits der Straße lockt noch immer die Ruhe weiter Almen und einsamer Gipfel jeden Schwierigkeitsgrades und in der freundlichen, weit auseinandergezogenen Siedlung wird sich jeder wohlfühlen.

Sehenswert im Ort und in der Umgebung

Die **Pfarrkirche zu den hll. Leonhard und Lampert** wurde 1730–1735 von Hans Holzmeister aus Hippach erbaut; die Deckenbilder stammen von Josef Michael Schmutzer aus Wessobrunn; die Altäre aus der Bauzeit wurden zum Teil erneuert, auf dem Hochalter eine Marienfigur von Josef Bachlechner (1911). – Der **Speicher Durlaßboden** an der Mündung des Wildgerlostales in das Gerlostal.

Spazierwege und Bergtouren

In das Schönachtal zur Stinkmoosalm (1348 m), ca. ¾ Std., weiter sanft ansteigend zur Jausenstation Lackenalm (1400 m), ½ Std. – Zur Issalm durch das Schönachtal und über die Pasteinalm (1692 m) in den innersten Talkessel, ca. 3 Std. – Nach Gmünd über die Gerlostalalm (1756 m) und am Waldweg zurück, ca. 4 Std. – In das Wimmertal bis zur Grundhütte (1685 m), von Gmünd, ca. 1½ – 2 Std. – Auf den Gerlospass (1531 m) am Zentralalpenweg (Variante) 02 über die Königsleitenalmen, 4 Std. – Auf den Schönbichl (2049 m), von Gerlos über die Kreidlschlagalm auf den breiten Rücken, mit dem der Schönachkamm nach Norden ausläuft; über diesen auf die aussichtsreiche Graskuppe, ca. 2½ Std. – Auf den Arbiskogel (2048 m), direkt von Gerlos südwärts, ca. 2½ Std. (bei Benützung der Fürstalmbahn zur Fürstalm, 1824 m, verkürzt sich die Gehzeit um 1½ Std.); dann Übergang zur Kirchspitze (2312 m), ¾ Std. (leicht); Abstieg eventuell über die Kothüttenalm nach Gmünd. – Zum Brandberger Kolmhaus (1845 m), vom Gasthaus Kühle Rast (Bushaltestelle) über das Brandberger Joch (2307 m), ca. 4 Std. – Auf den Isskogel (2268 m) über die Ebenfeldaste (1864 m); mit Benützung der Isskogelbahn, 1½ Std. – Zur Zittauer Hütte (2328 m) durch das Wildgerlostal; von Gerlos 6 Std., vom Gasthaus Finkau 3 Std.

GERLOSBERG   G 12

Gemeinde, Bezirk Schwaz, Einwohner: 460, Höhe: 1100 m, Postleitzahl: 6280. **Auskunft:** Tourismusverband Gerlos – Zell. **Bahnstation:** Zell am Ziller (5 km). **Busverbindung:** mit Zell am Ziller.

Die kleine Gemeinde bildete ursprünglich eine Hauptmannschaft des Salzburger Pflegerichtes Zell am Ziller und blieb dem führenden Talort bis zum heutigen Tag in vieler Hinsicht eng verbunden. Alle weiteren Angaben siehe daher dort.

Gesundheits-Tipp

Die Länge der Wanderung muss dem Leistungsvermögen der Teilnehmer angepasst werden.

ratiopharm

20

Gemeinde, Bezirk Schwaz, Einwohner: 670, Höhe: 944 m, Postleitzahl: 6280. **Auskunft:** Gemeindeamt Hainzenberg. **Bahnstation:** Zell am Ziller (5 km). **Busverbindung:** mit Zell am Ziller, Mayrhofen, Gerlos – Wald im Pinzgau. **Bergbahnen:** Gerlossteinbahn, Sessel- und Schlepplift am Arbiskögerl.

Am Fuße der mächtigen Gerlossteinwand liegt die Gemeinde Hainzenberg, die nach Süden an die Gemeinde Ramsau im Zillertal, im Osten an Gerlos, im Norden an Gerlosberg und im Nordwesten an Zell am Ziller anschließt. Die Gemeinde besteht überwiegend aus Streusiedlungen. Den Dorfkern bildet Hainzenberg, wo sich u. a. Gemeindeamt, Volksschule und Kindergarten befinden, ebenfalls die Talstation der Gerlossteinbahn.

Am Hainzenberg wurde von Anfang des 16. Jh. bis in das 19. Jh. Gold gewonnen. Näheres dazu erfahren Sie im Goldschaubergwerk. Heute leben die Einwohner von der Bewirtschaftung ihrer Bauernhöfe und dem Tourismus. Gemütliche Gasthöfe und Pensionen sind ebenfalls vorhanden. Der Ausbau der Bundesstraße hat auch gewisse Vorteile (Rundfahrten Zell am See, Lofer, Wörgl, Krimmler Wasserfälle, Pass Thurn und Kitzbühel).

Sehenswert im Ort und in der Umgebung

Im 1250 erbauten **Haus Unterflörler** ist die kunsthistorische, unter Denkmalschutz stehende, **Bergwerkkapelle** noch zu sehen. Der Berufssteinsucher und Schnitzer Walter Burgstaller (vulgo Wurzensepp) betreut diese Kapelle und dort ist auch eine umfangreiche **Mineraliensammlung** zu besichtigen. – Die **Schaukäserei** mit Kiosk und **Tierpark** befindet

sich in unmittelbarer Nähe (gern besuchtes Ausflugsziel). – Dort befindet sich auch der Ausgangspunkt für die Führungen in das **Goldschaubergwerk**. Während der ca. 1 stündigen Führung erfahren Sie Interessantes über die Arbeitsbedingungen unter Tage, den Lebensstil der Bergleute und ihr soziales Umfeld. – Die **Wallfahrtskapelle Maria Rast**, deren Vorläuferin die Kapelle zu Unterflörler war, ist sehr sehenswert. Spätgotisches Tor, vier spätgotische, nun restaurierte Fenster, Ausstattung aus dem 18. Jahrhundert; Stukkaturen und gute Deckenbilder von Josef Michael Schmutzer aus Wessobrunn, 1741; schöner Rokoko-Hochaltar von Stefan Föger, 1748, mit barockem Muttergottesbild; Kanzel ebenfalls (?) von Föger.

Goldschaubergwerk/Demonstration Gold Mine
Miniera d'oro aperta al pubblico

Spazierwege und Bergtouren

Nach Zell am Ziller über Maria Rast auf dem Waldweg, 1 Std. – Zum Gerlosstein-Berghotel (1620 m) von der letzten großen Kehre der Bundesstraße, ca. 2½ Std. oder vom Ötschenwirt, 2 Std. Das Gerlosstein-Berghotel ist auch mit der Gerlossteinbahn zu erreichen.

HIPPACH

F 12-13

Gemeinde, Bezirk Schwaz, Einwohner: 1380, Höhe: 608 m, Postleitzahl: 6283. **Auskunft:** Tourismusverband Hippach – Ramsau – Schwendau. **Bahnstation:** Ramsau-Hippach. **Busverbindung:** mit Jenbach, Mayrhofen, Gerlos – Wald im Pinzgau. **Bergbahnen:** siehe Mayrhofen.

Das stattliche Dorf bildet den Mittelpunkt der Tourismusgemeinden, die sich auf der Westseite des Hinteren Zillertales am Fuße des dicht besiedelten Schwendberges hinziehen. Der Ort wurde urkundlich erstmals Mitte des 13. Jahrhunderts erwähnt, doch sind Kirche und Siedlung sicherlich weit älter. Sein Name ist deutschen Ursprungs und weist auf die Lage an dem heute gebändigten Bach hin, der den deutlich erkennbaren Schwemmkegel zwischen Hippach und Schwendau aufschüttete. Schon Ende des 17. Jahrhunderts wurde Hippach durch eine heilkräftige Quelle als „Badl" bekannt. Seine Entwicklung zum modernen Tourismuszentrum verdankt es seiner sonnigen, verkehrsgünstigen Lage, seiner gepflegten Gastlichkeit und nicht zuletzt einer Reihe begabter und origineller Menschen, unter denen wir Sänger, bildende Künstler, Gelehrte und Persönlichkeiten des öffentlichen Lebens finden.

Sehenswert im Ort und in der Umgebung

Die ursprünglich gotische **Kirche zu den hll. Ingenuin und Albuin** wurde nach einem Erdbeben von 1699 erneuert und barockisiert. Aus der gotischen Zeit sind noch das in den östlichen Querarm verlegte Portal und der Turm an der Südseite. Stukkaturen, Ende des 17. Jahrhunderts; mittlere Deckenbilder aus dem späten 19. Jahrhundert; seitliche Fresken von Josef Michael Schmutzer aus Wessobrunn, 1746; ein seitliches Bild vom heimischen Künstler Matthäus Schiestl, 1914; von diesem und Johann Sporer die Statuen an den Seitenaltären; barocke Statuen am Hochaltar. – Besonders empfehlenswert ist eine Fahrt über die **Zillertaler Höhenstraße** (Maut!), von der aus auch schöne Wanderungen unternommen werden können. – Drei **Linden** werden als Naturdenkmal geschützt. – Empfehlenswert ist in **Laimach** ein Besuch im **Museum „Strasser Häusl"**.

In diesem denkmalgeschützten, gut erhaltenen, völlig aus Holz erbauten Zillertaler Bauernhaus aus dem 18. Jh., lebten einst die Geschwister Strasser und brachten von hier aus das Weihnachtslied „Stille Nacht, heilige Nacht" in die ganze Welt.

Spazierwege und Bergtouren

Nach Mayrhofen, entweder über die Zillerbrücke und längs des östlichen Ufers oder westlich über Stockach – Mühlbach – Burgstallschrofen, ca. 1 Std. – Nach Zell am Ziller über die Ziller-Promenade am Ostufer oder auf der Straße über Laimach – Zellbergeben, ca. 1 Std. – Zum Laimacher und Talbach-Wasserfall auf dem Prof.-Dr.-Rieser-Weg. Bei der Straßenkehre zweigt der markierte Weg zu den Wasserfällen ab; zurück über Laimach, 2 Std. – Zum Keiler-Wasserfall und über Schwendau zurück, ca. 2 Std. – Zum Gasthof Mösl, 2½ Std. – Zum Gschößwandhaus (1762 m), vom Gasthof Mösl, 1½ Std. – Zur Rastkogelhütte (2117 m), vom Gasthof Mösl, 2 Std.

MAYRHOFEN E 2/F 14

Marktgemeinde, Bezirk Schwaz, Einwohner: 3980, Höhe: 633 m, Postleitzahl: 6290. **Auskunft:** Tourismusverband Mayrhofen. **Bahnstation:** Mayrhofen. **Busverbindung:** mit Jenbach, zur Talstation der Hintertuxer Gletscherbahnen in Hintertux, Brandberg, Ginzling, Gerlos – Wald im Pinzgau, zum Bergrestaurant Schlegeis am Schlegeisspeicher, zum Gasthof Wasserfall am Speicher Stillup und zum Gasthof Bärenbad und weiter zum Speicher Zillergründl. In der Wintersaison Gratis-Schibus zu den Seilbahnen. **Bergbahnen:** Seilbahnen, Sessel- und Schlepplifte.

Mayrhofen ist eine der ältesten Tourismusorte Tirols. Die Urlaubsmetropole befindet sich im Talkessel des hinteren Zillertales, vor der imposanten Bergwelt des Naturparks Zillertaler Alpen. Mayrhofen gehörte bis 1801 zur Gemeinde Brandberg. Der Ort, einst bäuerliches Dörflein, war nur über sogenannte Saumwege aus dem Süden und eine schlechte Talstraße aus dem Norden zu erreichen.

Heute hingegen findet hier jeder wonach er sucht. Mayrhofen wurde zum Tourismuszentrum des Zillertals, aber trotz Weiterentwicklung und Modernisierung blieb der Charakter dieses Dorfes erhalten.

Sehenswert im Ort und in der Umgebung

Alte **Bauernhäuser** kann man im Ortsteil Haus und im nahen Brandberg bewundern. So zum Beispiel das 400 Jahre alte Bauernhaus zum Griena, das heute als uriges Wirtshaus dient und das, aus der 2. Hälfte des 17. Jh. stammende, Gratzerhaus. Liebhaber der modernen Kunst werden vom Karg Haus in der Scheulingstraße, dessen Fassade von der Tiroler Künstlerin Patrizia Karg gestaltet wurde, begeistert sein. – Auch die **Pfarrkirche „Unsere Liebe Frau"** in Mayrhofen, mit dem Deckengemälde „Die Rose von Jericho" von Max Weiler, ist für Kunstinteressierte zu empfehlen. – Alles Wissenswerte über Käsekultur, dem Leben auf der Alm und der Tradition der Einheimischen erfährt man in der **Erlebnis Sennerei Zillertal**. Seit dem Jahr 2000 wird hier auf einer Fläche von 6.000 m² den Besuchern die Welt der Milch- und Käseproduktion näher gebracht. – Im **Europahaus** vermittelt das **Alpenrelief** einen Einblick in die Zillertaler Bergwelt mit dem einzigartigen Naturpark Zillertaler Alpen und dient auch zur Planung von Wanderungen und Bergtouren. – **Naturpark Zillertaler Alpen**.

Spazierwege und Bergtouren

Zur Wallfahrtskapelle am Burgschrofen, vom Unteren Dorfplatz, ½ Std. – Nach Ramsau über den Weiler Durst und immer am Wald entlang über Laubichl – Hollenzen – Eckartau, 1 Std. – Nach Zimmereben, vom Mariensteig zweigt der Weg nach ca. 20 Min. Aufstieg nordwärts ab, vom Unteren Dorfplatz ca. 1 Std. – Zum Gasthof Zillergrund auf dem Fahrweg, ½ Std.; zurück auf dem unmittelbar bei der Brücke nach links abzweigenden Steig über Kumbichl, ¾ Std. – Zur Edelhütte (2238 m) entweder mit der Ahornbahn zur Hahnpfalz und von dort in einer Stunde zur Hütte oder von Mayrhofen über das Gasthaus Alpenrose und über die Fellenbergalm, ca. 4½ – 5 Std. – Zur Brandberger Wallfahrtskapelle durch den Scheulingwald, ¾ Std. – Von dieser rechts auf dem Fahrweg nach Brandberg, ¾ Std. – Nach Zell am Ziller über die Ziller-Promenade am östlichen Ufer, 2 Std. – Zum Gasthof Astegg über den Mariensteig, ca. 2 Std.; von dort Abstieg nach Finkenberg, ¾ Std. und auf dem Wiesenweg zurück, ca. 1 Std. – Zum Gasthof Lacknerbrunn (1006 m) über den Weiler Haus zum Weiler Schmelzhütten mit dem Kraftwerk Mayrhofen, wo der romantische Steig durch die Stillupklamm beginnt, der neben den Wasserfällen und schließlich steil durch den Wald emporführt und knapp unterhalb der Abzweigung zum Wiesenhof den Fahrweg erreicht, ca. 1½ Std. – Zum Wiesenhof (1058 m) zweigt man beim Gasthof Brücke links ab und erreicht über die schönen Höfe von Kumbichl einen Güterweg, der rechts in bequemer Steigung emporführt, oder man geht an dessen Abzweigung noch geradeaus auf dem Weg zur „Alpenrose" weiter von dem bald ein Waldweg rechts abzweigt, dem man folgt, ca. 1½ Std. – Zum Penkenhaus (1814 m), mit der Penkenbahn zur Bergstation und zum Ziel; zurück über den Gasthof Astegg, 3½ Std. – Auf den Rastkogel (2762 m) mit der Penkenbahn zur Bergstation und über die Wanglalm und die Wanglspitz (2420 m) auf den Gipfel. Am gleichen Weg retour, 6 Std. – Auf die Ahornspitze (2973 m), mit der Ahornbahn zur Hahnpfalz und über die Edelhütte (2238 m) auf den Gipfel, 3½ Std. – Zur Kasseler Hütte (2178 m) vom Gasthof Wasserfall, das beim Speicher Stillup liegt, auf Weg 515 zur Grüne-Wand-Hütte (1436 m) und zum Ziel, 2½ Std. – Weitere Vorschläge, insbesondere für Hochtouren siehe unter „Höhenwege" und „Alpengasthöfe und Unterkunftshütten".

RAMSAU im Zillertal   E 1/F 13

Gemeinde, Bezirk Schwaz, Einwohner: 1580, Höhe: 604, Postleitzahl: 6284. **Auskunft:** Tourismusverband Hippach – Ramsau – Schwendau. **Bahnstation:** Ramsau-Hippach. **Busverbindung:** mit Jenbach, Mayrhofen, Zell am Ziller, Gerlos – Wald im Pinzgau. **Bergbahnen:** Sessel- und Schlepplifte.

Die in der Gemeinde Ramsau zusammengefassten Siedlungen liegen an den Hängen des trotz starker Rodung noch immer waldreichen Ramsberges oder an dessen Fuß am Ostrand der Talsohle des Hinteren Zillertales. Tourismusmäßig ist Ramsau mit Hippach zusammengeschlossen. Der Ramsberg-Sessellift und zahlreiche bequeme Wege erschließen ein aussichtsreiches Wander- und Erholungsgebiet in luftiger Höhe.

Sehenswert im Ort und in der Umgebung

Die spätklassizistische **Pfarrkirche zu den Sieben Schmerzen Mariens**; den Hochaltar schmücken u. a. Statuen der hll. Isidor und Notburga aus dem Jahr 1770. – In **Oberbichl** das **Studio Alte Mühle** Max Hochmuths (vulgo Wurzelmax), der den Lebensunterhalt seiner großen Familie als Maler, Schnitzer, Musiker, Mineraliensammler und -händler und nicht zuletzt als „Zillertaler Original" bestreitet.

Spazierwege und Bergtouren

Nach Zell am Ziller über die Ziller-Promenade, 50 Min., oder am Fuß des Ramsberges über den Weiler Schweiber und zuletzt auf der Straße, 1 Std. – Nach Mayrhofen über die Ziller-Promenade oder über die Weiler Unter- und Oberbichl, Eckartau und Hollenzen, teils durch Lindenwald, 1 Std. – Nach Mayrhofen über die Bergstation des Ramsberglifts, die Kotahornalm und das Berggasthaus Steinerkogl (1270 m), 4 ½ – 5 Std. – Zur Mittelstation des Sessellifts, von Ramsau über die Jausenstation Waldheim, 1 Std. – Zum Gerlosstein-Berghotel (1620 m) über die Bergstation des Ramsberglifts, 2 Std.

ROHRBERG   G 11

Gemeinde, Bezirk Schwaz, Einwohner: 520, Höhe: ca. 1000 m, Postleitzahl: 6280. **Auskunft:** Tourismusverband Zell – Gerlos. **Bahnstation:** Zell am Ziller, von Rohr (1½ km). Alles Weitere siehe Zell am Ziller.

Die kleine Bergbauerngemeinde besteht vorwiegend aus Streusiedlungen, die im Zuge des mittelalterlichen Siedlungsausbaus durch Rodung entstanden.

Spazierwege und Bergtouren: siehe Zell am Ziller.

SCHWENDAU   E 1/F 13

Gemeinde, Bezirk Schwaz, Einwohner: 1550, Höhe: 620 m, Postleitzahl: 6283. **Auskunft:** Tourismusverband Hippach – Ramsau – Schwendau. **Bahnstation:** Ramsau-Hippach (ca. 0,2 km). **Busverbindung:** siehe Hippach. **Bergbahn:** siehe Mayrhofen.

Schwendau liegt am Rande der sonnigen Talweitung nahe der Mündung des Sidanbaches in das Haupttal. Sidan- und Hoarbergbach haben sich tief in die weichen Quarzphyllite eingeschnitten und durch die starke Geschiebeführung einen breiten Schwemmkegel aufgeschüttet, durch den der Ziller nach Osten gedrängt wird. Der Name der Siedlung wird erstmals um 1200 als Swentouwe im Urbar des Erzstiftes Salzburg erwähnt und belegt ebenso wie die Ortsnamen Schwendberg und Stockach die umfangreiche Rodungsarbeit der Siedlungsgründer. Schwendau ist die Heimat des 1934 verstorbenen Bauerndoktors Kiendler, dessen Ruf weit über die Grenzen des Tales, ja sogar bis nach Japan reichte. Von seinen originellen Heilpraktiken weiss man sich heute noch zu erzählen, manche werden wohl noch heute angewendet und weitergegeben.

Sehenswert im Ort und in der Umgebung

Die **Kapelle zum Gekreuzigten Heiland** am Burgstallschrofen wurde 1844 erbaut. – Der **Keiler-Wasserfall**. – **Brennhütte**. – **Schaumühle Zimmerhäusl**. – **Alte Bauernhöfe**. – **Dorfkapelle**. – **Johann-Sponring-Brunnen**.

Spazierwege

Nach Hippach, ½ Std. – Nach Mayrhofen auf der Ziller-Promenade über Mühlbach, Burgstall und Burgstallschrofen, ¾ Std. – Zum Keiler-Wasserfall, 1 Std. – Zum Gasthof Zimmereben, von Burgstall, ca. 50 Min.; Abstieg unter Umständen nach Mayrhofen oder Finkenberg. – Nach Burgstall auf dem Schwendauer Waldweg über Mühlen und auf der Ziller-Promenade zurück, ca. 1½ Std.

TUX BC 2-4

Gemeinde, Bezirk Schwaz, Einwohner: 1920, Höhe: 1300 – 3476 m, Postleitzahl: 6293. **Auskunft:** Tourismusverband Tux – Finkenberg. **Bahnstation:** Mayrhofen (14 km). **Busverbindung:** mit Mayrhofen und bis zur Talstation der Hintertuxer Gletscherbahnen in Hintertux. **Bergbahnen:** Hintertuxer Gletscherbahnen: Wandern und Sommer- und Winterskilauf möglich (Seilbahnen, Sessel- und Schlepplifte), Eggalmbahn (4-er Gondelbahn).

Am Ende des Zillertales zweigt von Mayrhofen (633 m) das Tuxer Tal ab. Eine kurvenreiche, aber gut ausgebaute Straße führt zuerst nach Finkenberg (839 m) und überquert mit der mächtigen Rosengartenbrücke die Tuxbachklamm. Von dort sind es nur mehr 4 km bis zum Erreichen der Gemeindegrenze von Tux – hier beginnt „s' Tux an schian Tal". Wer also, wie die Tuxer sagen „ins Tux" fährt, findet heutzutage gute, sichere Verkehrswege. Die Gemeinde Tux liegt auf einer Seehöhe von 1257 m (Vorderlanersbach) bis 1493 m (Hintertux). Die höchste Erhebung ist der Olperer mit 3476 m. Die 5 Orte der Gemeinde Tux – Hintertux, Madseit, Juns, Lanersbach und Vorderlanersbach – erstrecken sich über 8 km, und ganzjährig fühlen sich Gäste und Einheimische im idyllischen Tuxer Tal wohl. Bis zur Mitte des 15. Jh. gehörte Hintertux zur Pfarre Matrei im Wipptal. Erst 1926 löst sich Hintertux von der Gemeinde Schmirn. Seither bilden die ehemalige salzburgische Hofmark Lanersbach, die Hauptmannschaft Lämperbichl und Hintertux die heutige Gemeinde Tux.

Tux ist auch geologisch gesehen von Bedeutung, da es die Gesteinsscheide zwischen den Tuxer Alpen (Tonschiefergebirge) und dem Tuxer Hauptkamm (granitartiger Gneis) bildet. Am schönen Talschluss in Hintertux erhebt sich der mächtige Hintertuxer Gletscher mit dem Olperer, 3476 m, der höchsten Erhebung des Tales. Der verschiedenartige Aufbau der Gebirge auf beiden Talseiten gibt Tux seinen ganz besonderen landschaftlichen Reiz und verteilt seine Schönheiten gleichermaßen an die Freunde des Bergwanderns wie an jene der Hochalpinistik.

Durch die geschützte Lage ist das Klima in Tux bedeutend günstiger, als es seine Höhenlage und Gletschernähe vermuten lässt und die Hänge sind bis an den Rand des Gletschers grün – daher spricht man vom „Grünen Gletschertal". Langjährige Mittelwerte aus Tux, erhoben von der Wetterwarte Innsbruck. Pro Jahr gibt es in Tux: 1839 Sonnenstunden, 12 Nebeltage und 153 Tage mit Schnee im Tal.

Sehenswert im Ort und in der Umgebung

Von Juni bis September wird jeden Montag von 13 – 16 Uhr Korn in der **Tuxer Mühle** in **Juns** gemahlen. – In **Madseit** das **Mehlerhaus**, ein Bauernhaus aus dem 17. Jh., das bis 1992 bewohnt war und 1999 von der Gemeinde Tux renoviert und für Besucher zugänglich gemacht wurde. Die alten Stuben und die Küche können am Montag von 14 – 17 Uhr besichtigt werden. – In der **Höllensteinhütte** befindet sich das **Bäuerliche Museum**, das Aufschluss über das harte Leben der Bergbauern und Holzarbeiter in Tux gibt. – **Talwanderweg zu den „Drei Kreuzen"** in **Hintertux**. – Nahe dem **Spannagelhaus**, 2531 m (10 Minuten von der Bergstation/Sektion II der Hintertuxer Gletscherbahnen entfernt) liegt die seit 1964 als Naturdenkmal geschützte **Spannagelhöhle**. Die Höhle ist 4,2 km lang und bis zu 25 m tief. Sie ist die größte Höhle Tirols und bietet vor allem auch einen Einblick in die hochalpine Verkarstung der Gletscherregionen. Dauer des Rundganges 1 Stunde. Besichtigung mit Führung im Sommer und Winter möglich! – **Denkmalgeschützte Bauernhöfe** aus dem 18. Jh. in **Gemais** oberhalb von Vorderlanersbach. – Beim **ehemaligen Magnesitwerk** auf der Schrofenalm die **Kapelle zur hl. Barbara** mit dem wunderschönen Fresko des Malers

Max Weiler. – Die auf 1984 m Seehöhe gelegene Junsalm mit der **Jausenstation** und **Bergkäserei Stoankasern**; von Mitte Juni bis Ende September kann man zusehen, wie die Milch zu Butter und Käse verarbeitet wird. – **Pfarrkirchen** und **Kapellen** in den **Ortsteilen**. – Am Talabschluss in Hintertux stürzen unterhalb der Gefrorenen-Wand-Spitze tosend die **Tuxer Wasserfälle** in tiefe Felsenkessel. So wird der Schraubenwasserfall bereits seit dem Jahr 1964 als Naturdenkmal geschützt. Am Weg zum Tuxer Joch kommen Sie beim Schleierwasserfall vorbei.

Wanderungen und Bergtouren
250 km markierte Wege zu Alpenblumen, Seen, bewirtschafteten Hütten und Gipfeln. Hochgebirgstouren, Themenwege und geführte Wanderungen mit 3 – 7 Stunden Gehzeit. • **Tipp**: Wasserfallweg (Rundtour, ca. 1½ Stunden); Moorlehrpfad, 2 Std; Themenweg mit 9 Informationstafeln (Klima, Wasser, Geologie, Bergwald, Lawinen, Lärche und Fichte, Alm, Gletscher und Trockensteinmauer); dieser 1 km lange Weg verbindet den Ortskern von Hintertux mit dem Parkplatz der Hintertuxer Gletscherbahn.

Wanderservice: Seilbahnen und Wandertaxi als Aufstiegshilfen für Traum-Panorama, kostenloser Wanderbus. Erlebnis Gletscher mit Eisbruchquerung und Klettern. Bergsportschule und Bergführer, Natursport Tirol mit Canyoning, Höhlentrekking, Flying Fox, Kraxel-Maxel-Camp, etc.

Genusswandern vom Spaziergang bis zur anspruchsvollen Hochgebirgstour; 17 Jausenstationen bzw. Schutzhütten (Bewirtschaftungszeit von Juni bis Oktober)

Tourenvorschläge
Bergstation Eggalm (1948 m) – Grüblspitze (2395 m) – Torsee – Lanersbach, 5 Std. – Bergstation Eggalm (1948 m) – Waldhoar – Brandalm – Lanersbach, 2½ Std. – Sommerbergalm – Frauenwand – Tuxer-Joch-Haus (2310 m) – Weitental – Hintertux, 4 Std. – Hintertux – Spannagelhaus (2531 m), wenige Minuten entfernt die Spannagelhöhle, mit der Gondelbahn retour, 3 Std. – Lämmerbichl – Rastkogel (2762 m) – Vorderlanersbach, 6 Std. – Bergkäserei Stoankasern – Junsjoch (2484 m) – Juns, 5 Std.

ZELL am Ziller   F 11

Marktgemeinde, Bezirk Schwaz, Einwohner: 1770, Höhe: 575 m, Postleitzahl: 6280. **Auskunft:** Tourismusverband Zell – Gerlos. **Bahnstation:** Zell am Ziller. **Busverbindung:** mit Jenbach und Mayrhofen und Gerlos – Wald im Pinzgau. **Bergbahnen:** Gondelbahnen, Sessel- und Schlepplifte.

Zell am Ziller konnte sich dank seiner günstigen Mittellage unmittelbar südlich der Talenge, die das untere Zillertal vom oberen scheidet, zum lebhaften Hauptort des ganzen Tales entwickeln. Die Siedlung erstreckt sich über die weite Talsohle beiderseits des Zillers. Wie der Name erkennen lässt, befand sich hier schon sehr früh ein kleines Kloster mit Kirche (cella = Zelle), deren Besitzungen auf die Siedlung übertragen wurden. Diese wird bereits in dem ältesten Urbar des Erzstiftes Salzburg (um 1200) als einer der Haupthöfe des Amtes Zillertal angeführt. Zell wurde später Sitz des Pflege- und Propsteigerichtes und wird seit dem 12. Jahrhundert als eine der beiden salzburgischen Urpfarren des Zillertales erwähnt. Als Gerichts-, Dekanats- und Behördensitz, sowie durch seine Gewerbe- und Dienstleistungsbetriebe besitzt es auch heute für das Tal zentrale Bedeutung. Alljährlich Anfang Mai wird hier das älteste Frühlingsfest Tirols, das „Gauderfest" mit Musik und Tanz, Ranggeln und Widderstoßen, mit Gauderwürsten und Gauderbier gefeiert. Letzteres wird eigens in der seit dem Jahr 1500 bestehenden Brauerei des Ortes hergestellt, deren Besitzer vor rund 400 Jahren das Fest ins Leben gerufen haben. Die urwüchsige Fröhlichkeit der Zillertaler kann man in Zell auch noch bei anderen Gelegenheiten miterleben, so im Fasching, beim Almabtrieb oder bei dem weit und breit berühmten Zeller Kirchtag, der jährlich am 15. August (Maria Himmelfahrt) stattfindet.

Sehenswert im Ort und in der Umgebung

Von der wohl aus dem 14. Jahrhundert stammenden **Pfarrkirche zum hl. Veit** blieb nur der gotische Westturm erhalten; an ihn wurde Ende des 18. Jahrhunderts von A. Hueber eine schöne Rokoko-Zentralanlage nach Plänen W. Hagenauers angeschlossen; Freskenfragment an der Westseite der Vorhalle; Deckengemälde um 1500; Hochaltarbild (hl. Veit) und vermutlich auch die Seitenaltarblätter von Franz Anton Zeiller, 1779; Taufstein mit spätbarocker Schnitzgruppe in der Vorhalle; am Friedhof Wappensteingrab von Johann Schoner mit Gemahlin, gestorben 1451. – **Wallfahrtskapelle Maria Rast, Schaukäserei, Tierpark und Goldschaubergwerk:** siehe **Hainzenberg**.

Spazierwege und Bergtouren

Siehe auch Anschlussblatt, KOMPASS-Wanderkarte 28 „Vorderes Zillertal – Alpbach – Rofan – Wildschönau".

Rundgang vom Dorfplatz auf der Kraus-Promenade, von der Rohrerstraße zur Gerlosstraße, insgesamt ca. 1 Std. – Nach Mayrhofen über die Ziller-Promenade längs des östlichen Ziller-Ufers, 2 Std.; zurück unter Umständen über die Dörfer Schwendau, Hippach und Laimach. – Zur Wallfahrtskirche Maria Rast auf dem Weg Nummer 7, ca. 1½ Std. – Zum Gerlosstein-Berghotel (1620 m) vom Ötschenwirt (Autobushaltestelle) oder von der letzten großen Kehre vor Hainzenberg direkt durch den Wald, ca. 2 – 2½ Std.; von dort viele Wanderungen möglich, wie zur Gerlossteinwand (2166 m), 1½ – 2 Std.; zum Arbiskögerl (1830 m), 1 Std.; nach Mayrhofen über die Kotahorn- und Labergalm und das Berggasthaus Steinerkogl, ca. 3 Std.

ZELLBERG   F 11

Gemeinde, Bezirk Schwaz, Einwohner: 650, Höhe: 580 – 1000 m, Postleitzahl: 6280. **Auskunft:** Tourismusverband Zell – Gerlos. Alles weitere siehe Zell am Ziller.

Die Streusiedlungen des Zellberges bildeten eine Hauptmannschaft des Salzburger Pfleggerichtes Zell, kirchlich gehört es jedoch zur Pfarre Hippach, da der Ziller die Diözesan- und Pfarrgrenze bildet.

Wir möchten Sie auf den KOMPASS-Wanderführer Zillertal, Verlagsnummer 903, hinweisen.

Eine Möglichkeit zur Orientierung ist das **GPS** (Global Positioning System). Mit einem GPS-Gerät kann man weltweit seine Position (Angabe in Koordinaten) bestimmen. Möglich ist dies durch Satelliten, die die Erde in etwa 20.200 km Höhe mit einer Geschwindigkeit von ca. 11.200 km/h umkreisen und laufend Signale senden. Verwendet man ein GPS, muss man das MapDatum und das zugrunde liegende Ellipsoid des jeweiligen Landes in Erfahrung bringen, weil man sonst falsche Koordinatenangaben erhält. Der Umgang mit einem GPS-Gerät verlangt allerdings ein sehr gutes Wissen im Kartenlesen und vor allem Übung im Handling.

KOMPASS Hiking Map 1:25000, sheet No. 037 „Mayrhofen – Tux Valley – Zillergrund" deals with the Alps centered around the famous resort town Mayrhofen. Numerous headwater valleys converge here from all sides to form the broad main valley, the Zillertal, that strikes a course almost due north to the Inn Valley. At Zell am Ziller (on the northern perimeter of the map) it is joined on the east by the water-rich Gerlos Valley. These long feeder valleys, the so-called 'innere Gründe' or inner valleys, are the passageways to the spectacular mountain world surrounding the upper Ziller Valley.

The small valleys extending southward to the main body of the Alps are excellent for hiking to the Alpine Club's spacious huts at the valley's head. Zillergrund (taxi bus service) starts east of Mayrhofen and forks to form Zillergründl, Hundskehlgrund and Sundergrund. To the south, the main valley takes a step down to Stillupgrund (toll road to the reservoir). From Ginzling, Floitengrund leads to the very heart of the Ziller Valley Alps. Gunggl, Zemmgrund and Schlegeisgrund lay in a row, before Zamser Grund climbs to Pfitscher Joch (2248 m) and the Italian border. Between the Zams and Tux valleys is the main chain of the Tux Alps (Tuxer Hauptkamm), with Olperer Mountain (3476 m) one of the most prominent peaks east of Brenner Pass. The peak can be seen for miles. Starting at Finkenberg, the Tux Valleys forms the gateway to the Tux Alps and the year-round ski resort on Tuxer Ferner (glacier). The are two ways to cross Gerlos Pass (1531 m) to Wald im Pinzgau in the Upper Salzach Valley: take either the scenic toll road (view of the world-famous Krimmler Waterfalls) by way of Krimml, or the toll-free road that goes past Almdorf Königsleiten.

Geology

The Zillertal Alps with the Tuxer and Zillertaler Hauptkamm and the Reichenspitz Group work their beauty through the boldly postured somber crests and peaks strikingly contrasted with the icy sheen of the 'Keese' (glaciers), whose frothing brooks plunge to the valley below. Just south, on the other hand, is a completely different scene, that of the glacier-free foothills of the Tux Alps. This dissimilarity is the product of the region's geological make-up that can be broken down into the following units, generally striking from west to east.

The core of the Zillertal Alps is primarily composed of hard gneisses. This central gneiss zone starts in the west with the two arms of the Tuxer and Zillertaler Hauptkamm merging to form the Stilluppe before it continues east into the Hohe Tauern. The zone's southern limits span the length of the Ahrn Valley in South Tyrol, stretching to Eisbruggjoch in the west. Its northern border traces a line from Kraxentrager to Kaserer, Mayrhofen and Krimml. The gneiss core is encased on both sides by schist that juts in between the two gneiss arms in the west. Running close to the map's north edge, the northern periphery travels from Matrei in the Wipp Valley through Hippach to Gerlos Pass. The schist layer consists of all manner of rocks, particularly crystalline schists, and is divided into a lower zone of essentially non-calcareous rocks, that is closer to the central gneiss, as well as an upper or outer, largely calcareous zone. Hikers are sure to enjoy the rich abundance of minerals waiting to be found. Best known are the garnets, which were discovered at Rossrugg and crushed in a small garnet mill on the brook below Berliner Hütte. Under the influence of erosion, the hard, resistant gneisses were carved into daring peaks and knife-sharp crests, that still rose defiantly above the mighty glaciers that filled valleys and even flooded and leveled the summits of the Tux Alps during the Ice Age. On their travels the ice masses gouged deep valleys, creating the typical 'Trogtal' or U-shaped valley form, a term coined by glaciologists here in the Zillertal Alps, one of the earliest Alpine areas researched. Today the vast cirques to the north still feed the mighty glaciers, making them important natural reservoirs of hydroelectric power. The mountains' uncommonly steep south face permitted only limited glacial formation. Large deposits of weathering residue collected on the slopes and valley floor to be caught up by the brooks and washed away, while mudflows and floods repeatedly raged through the Zillertal. Ever since the Schlegeis, Stillup and Zillergründl reservoirs were constructed, flood disasters have been a thing of the past for the Ziller Valley.

History

Up to the Italian border, the entire area covered by this map belongs to Schwaz County in the northern Tyrol, with the exception of Schmirn Township of Greater Innsbruck County in the west. In 1926 the county line was pushed back to Tuxer Joch. In the southwest, St. Jakob Township in the Pfitsch Valley (Sterzing/Vipiteno County) lost its territory north of Pfitscher Joch following World War I. The Ahrn Valley is associated with the Puster Valley, centered around Bruneck/Brunico. Its ties spanning Hörndljoch, Hundskehljoch and Heilig-Geist-Jöchl to the inner Ziller Valley and its side valleys date from very early times, which accounts for the fact that the region's summer pastures are still owned by today's Ahrn Valley farmers although they long ago became part of the Ziller Valley for political and tax purposes.

The only prehistoric find in the region, a bronze needle, was made on Tuxer Joch, something that would appear to support this theory although it is certainly not sufficient proof. The map's east portion showing Krimml belongs to Salzburg's Zell am See County.

Research into the towns' names has shown that Illyrians, who were later romanized, also settled in the Ziller Valley. Relatively few in number, they were completely assimilated by the Baiuvarii, who entered the valley as of the 6th century. The influential role of these Bavarians in setling the valley is documented by the large number of towns and villages whose names refer to land clearing work. The first written mention of the Ziller Valley was made in the year 889 in a deed in which Arnulf, also duke of Bavaria, granted considerable lands in the 'Cilarestal' to Pilgrim, later archbishop of Salzburg. However, property lines and county lines did not coincide here. In Roman times the Ziller River formed the border between Rhaetia and Noricum and for centuries has marked the boundary between two counties. The county west of the river was ruled by the bishops of Brixen since the 11th century, from whom it passed to the Counts of Andechs and, after they died out, to the Hirschbergers; in 1263 and 1282 it finally entered the hands of the Counts of Tyrol. The eastern part of this county was conferred by the Counts of Andechs on their vassals, the Lords of Rottenburg, whose ancestral castle stood near Jenbach. This evolved into Rottenburg regional court, that held full jurisdiction up to its east border on the Ziller. The county east of the river extended to Kufstein and Erl and was ruled by the Bavarian counts of Rapoton, the bishops of Regensburg and, as of 1205, the House of Wittelsbach, whose 'county in the mountains' grew into the Kufstein, Kitzbühel and Rattenberg regional courts. The last of these presided over the land up to the Ziller. From 1290 to 1380 it was pledged as security to the sovereigns of Tyrol, who finally acquired it together with Kitzbühel and Kufstein in 1504 through Emperor Maximilian I. However, the archbishops of Salzburg were able to almost completely consolidate their sovereignty over the Ziller Valley holdings. As early as the 12th century a special office was set up to administer the Zillertal lands and from about 1200 on, the archbishopric itself exercised the bailiwick rights. As a defense measure, the archbishopric had Kropfsberg Castle erected at the mouth of the valley toward the end of the 13th century; its burgraves thenceforth served as the archbishop's highest official for the Zillertal.

Over the centuries, the closely interwoven properties and rights repeatedly gave rise to conflicts between Salzburg and Tyrol. The rulers of Tyrol claimed not only the assizes jurisdiction in the court districts growing out of these counties, but also the economically important forest, hunting and mining regalities. In actual fact, however, the archbishops of Salzburg exercised almost all the royal prerogatives in their estates on both banks of the Ziller with the exception of the high assizes, while constantly ignoring the jurisdiction of the Rottenburg and Rattenberg regional courts. The Tyroleans were able to at least partially realize their claims with regard to the exercies of royal prerogatives. With secularization of all of Germany's church-ruled principalities in 1803, the Archbishopric of Salzburg fell to the Habsburgs; it first entered the hands of the Habsburg's Tuscan line and in 1805 became an outright part of the Austrian Empire. Simultaneously, however, by relinquishing Tyrol its share of the Zillertal was lost to Bavaria. Consequently, the same rivalry continued over the regalities, but this time with new players. Salzburg's former towns voluntarily took an active part in Tyrol's 1809 Freedom Fight and an agreement was made with them by Andreas Hofer to unite the entire Ziller Valley with Tyrol. This union took place but under Bavarian sovereignty, since Austria's defeat meant that Salzburg, too, was ceded to Bavaria. The situation, however, was of short duration because the Congress of Vienna forced Bavaria to return all its newly acquired lands to Austria. In 1816 Emperor Francis I decreed that Salzburg's portion of the Zillertal and the Brixen Valley would finally be annexed to Tyrol. The news was greeted with joy by a population that had apparently always felt a common bond. In church matters, the valley remains divided to this day. The Ziller still remains the diocesan border. The parishes on the right bank of the river have green church towers and belong to Salzburg Diocese, while those on the left bank have red church towers and belong to Innsbruck Diocese.

Poor living conditions long ago led people to leave the valley, at a time when farming provided only a spartan existence for the growing population. Traders from the Ziller Valley ranged far and wide throughout the country. While records from the 16th century show that surplus goods, especially farm products such as lard, cheese and livestock, found markets in nearby areas, trade gradually expanded to other wares. Zillertaler schnaps has always been a popular drink, with its production and distribution earning a living for root diggers, distillers and traders. Especially well knwon were the Zillertal glove dealers, whose wares were generally not produced in the valley. The 17th and 18th centuries saw the 'Ölträger' do a booming trade in all sorts of ointments, oils and tinctures for man and beast alike, with many a customer getting a good shake-down for nothing short of quackery. In 1837 after the Tyrolean parliament chose not to recognize Emperor Joseph II's Edict of Tolerance, more than 400 persons had to leave their homes in Finkenberg and Brandberg rather than yield on matters of conscience and religion. They settled as a group in Prussian Silesia, where they founded a new town named 'Zillertal' that was a home away home for these Tyroleans until they were again expelled in 1945. These steadfast emigrants evoked the entire continent's admiration and helped make a name for the Ziller Valley. As early as the 1820s, when tourism had already discovered the Zillertal, singing ensembles and families such as the Rainers, Leos, Strassers and Hollaus popularized their home valley throughout the rest of Europe. The birth of alpinism and the new accessibility of the Alps in the mid 18th century gave tourism a major impetus and today tourism supplements agriculture as the foundation of the valley's economy. The valley has no industry at all; only recently have several larger businesses developed in some of the Zillertal's more sizeable towns without noticeable disturbance to their surroundings. The countryside, however, experienced considerable disruption in the wake of power plant construction, which caused the valley to lose its virgin appearance. New attractions in the valley are the Schlegeis, Stillup and Zillergründl reservoirs. The mines that used to be so widespread are almost all abandoned now. The gold mine on Hainzenberg was worked until the second half of the 19th century; today it is a tourist attraction. The garnet deposit on Rossrugg was discovered in the mid 18th century by a poaching farmer; the stones were system-atically collected for almost a hundred years, cleaned in the above-mentioned garnet mill in Zemmgrund and sold to Bohemian stone cutters. Production ceased in 1836. Only the old copper mine at Prettau in the Ahrn Valley was reopened on a modest scale from 1959 to 1971; today it is the South Tyrol Provincial Mining Museum/Prettau Demonstration Mine. The exploration and dressing of the magnesite and scheelite deposits tapped above Lanersbach after World War I provided employment for several hundred workers until the works closed in 1976.

Schlegeis Reservoir/Schlegeisspeicher/Bacino artificiale Schlegeis

The pretty traditional costume – black velvet bodice with pale silk scarf and matching apron atop a black skirt for women and girls, black leather breeches and gray loden jacket trimmed in black worn over a white shirt and red breast strap for men, with both sexes wearing a fetching black hat with gold tassel – is still worn on many festive occasions, both religious and non-religious.

Flora und Fauna

The Zillertal's inhabitants are born with a passion for hunting. The ibex that once thrived in the inner valleys has been completely wiped out, while the last rock goats were resettled outside the valley in the early 18th century by the Archbishop of Salzburg. Chamois, on the other hand, is still plentiful. Deer are particularly abundant in Gerlos Valley, where they can be watched at feeding time just outside town. Although the marmot's whistle-like call can still be heard in secluded areas, he is very seldom seen. Deer can be found from the valley floor to the tree line, the capercaillie and black grouse throughout the whole valley. The crystal-clear brooks abounding with trout are a joy for every angler. Despite the forest clearing formerly undertaken in the Zillertal, the valley is still sumptuously wooded. The most prevalent tree is the spruce, with the arolla pine predominating in the upper reaches of the wooded slopes. The local plant life covers a wide range of species including most of the better known Alpine flowers, whose habitats are dictated by climate and soil conditions. As everywhere throughout Tyrol, the rarest species are protected. Special protection has also been extended to Scheulingwald at Mayrhofen, the stand of linden trees near Ramsau and the mixed linden and beech wood called „Glocke" (with nature trail) in Finkenberg.

Long-Distance Hiking Trails

For information on all European long-distance hiking trails contact the „Weitwanderer Branch" of the Austrian Alpine Club: Thaliastrasse 159/3/16, 1160 Vienna/Austria, Fax and Tel.: ++43 (0)1 493 84 08 or cell phone: ++43 (0)664 273742
weitwanderer@sektion.alpenverein.at
www.alpenverein.at/weitwanderer • www.fernwege.de

The various Alpine Clubs have set up a network of marked long trails that are designated by a number and a name. This is intended to present destinations that were rarely visited before and to explore the great range of tourism possibilities.

For these trails special „hiking guides" have been brought out to familiarize hikers with the routes, lodgings opportunities, distances and elevations, hiking times and difficulty as well as the opening times for inns and Alpine huts. Moreover, stamp stations have been introduced where the hiker can stop for a stamp to prove he hiked that particular trail. After having collected a certain number of stamps, the hiker qualifies for various hiking pins, whereby it is not important how much time was needed for each trail.

In addition to numerous regional hiking trails, Austria has **ten long-distance hiking trails** numbered 01 to 10. A numeral preceding the trail number identifies the mountains where the trail is located. In the Central Alps this numeral is odd (for example, 702), while in the Northern and Southern Calcareous Alps it is even (for example, 801). A letter following the trail number (for example, 702A) means the trail is an alternative route (Variante). Numerous national long-distance trails have been incorporated into the international European Long-Distance Hiking Trail Network.

KOMPASS Map 037 shows Central Alpine Trail 02 (Zentralalpenweg 02).

Before setting out on your hike, please inquire whether the mentioned huts and towns provide lodgings. The long-distance hiking trails require Alpine experience, good physical condition and good equipment.

> **Alpine Emergency Signals:** Give a visual or acoustic signal **six times per minute** at regular intervals. Wait one minute. Repeat until a reply is received.
>
> **Reply:** Visual or acoustic signal given **three times per minute** at regular intervals.

Trail Descriptions
Central Alpine Trail 02/Main Trail (502) – Zentralalpenweg 02/Hauptweg (502):

Central Alpine Trail 02 begins in Hainburg an der Donau and runs to Feldkirch in Vorarlberg, traversing all of Austria's states except Upper Austria and Vienna. It is the most Alpine of all the long-distance trails and is 1,000 km long. Since this trail leads largely along higher elevations (some glacier crossings!), Alpine experience, good physical condition and good equipment are musts! Certified mountain guides can be hired in the valley towns to accompany you on a safe hike; inquire at the local Tourist Office. Before starting out on your hike, please inquire as to the current condition of the trails and whether sleeping quarters are available at the huts.

The trail enters the map from the right (K 17), coming from the Warnsdorfer Hütte, and crosses Zillerplattenscharte to reach the Plauener Hütte. Next, go past the Zillergründl Reservoir and take the road out of the valley until you pass four inns: Bärenbad, In der Au, Häusling and Klaushof. Now you are near Mayrhofen, from where you follow the road into the Stillup Reservoir, up to the Stilluphaus and Grüne-Wand-Hütte, and up the steep trail to the Kasseler Hütte. Make a wide arc around several 3,000-m peaks, where there is one glacier after another, up to Lapenscharte and down to the Greizerhütte. The trail continues down to Floitengrund and then climbs ladders (hikers must be surefooted and have no fear of heights) up the steep trail to Mörchenscharte, and just as steeply to Rosskar and Schwarzensee (lake) until it finally reaches the Berliner Hütte. The trail proceeds tediously along an exposed, cable-secured stretch along Schönbichler Grat and on then along Berliner Höhenweg to the Furtschaglhaus. Follow the hairpin curves down to Schlegeisgrund and take the road along the Schlegeis Reservoir to Zamser Grund. Central Alpine Trail 02 then branches off to climb to the Olperer Hütte. It continues over steep and tedious terrain across Riepengrat to Alpeiner Scharte and, in a descent demanding extreme caution, down to the Geraer Hütte, where it leaves the map (A 7) in the direction of Vals.

Central Alpine Trail/Zentralalpenweg 02 – Alternative/Variante (702A, 502A, 302A)
The alternative route was created to bypass difficult and very difficult portions of the Main Trail. This trail also runs largely at high elevations (some glacier crossings!), and therefore demands Alpine experience, good physical condition and good equipment (see remarks for Main Trail)! On this map Central Alpine Trail 02 is paralleled by an alternative route (702A, 502A, 302A) from Almdorf Königsleiten, where the trail enters the map at the upper right-hand side (K 11) to pass Gerlos, Gmünd, Hainzenberg and Maria Rast to Hippach. Take Zillertaler-Höhenstrasse to Grün, where the trail leaves the map for the first time in the direction of the Rastkogelhütte (D 1) only to return from the same hut and reenter the map at C 1. The trail follows the upper edge of the map over Rastkogel, before it turns toward the Weidener Hütte (B 1) and again leaves the map. It enters the map a last time at A 1, where it crosses Krovenzjoch on its way to the Lizumer Hütte at the Lizum-Walchen military training ground, continues to Geier and Lizumer Rechner, shortly after which it leaves the map at A 3 in the direction of Navis.

Restricted Areas:
In an effort to promote compatibility between hunting and forestry interests and the many people who enjoy hiking, cycling and mountain climbing, the Austrian Alpine Club (www.alpenverein.or.at/naturschutz (Bergsport und Umwelt), Tel. ++43/(0)512/59547) has prepared a databank of all the areas restricted in Austria for hunting, forestry or military purposes as well as game preserves and all major nature, landscape and special preserves. KOMPASS-Karten GmbH thanks the Austrian Alpine Club for the information it so kindly provided for this KOMPASS hiking map.

High Trails

Tux Alps
Crossings are also recommended for ski touring, provided there is no danger of avalanches.
Day 1:
a) Start at Penken Cable Car mountain station or Gschößwandhaus; by foot from Mayrhofen, 3 – 3½ hrs.; cross Gschößberg to Penkenjochhaus (2095 m), 1¼ hrs.; continue to Wanglalm, then over Wanglspitz (2420 m) and Hoarbergjoch (2590 m), from here over boulder gravel to the top of the Rastkogel (2762 m), total 3½ – 4 hrs.
b) Start at Rastkogelhütte, which is reached from Hippach in 4 – 4½ hrs. or from Gasthaus Mösl (inn at bus stop) in approx. 1½ – 2 hrs.: climb from the hut to Rastkogel (2762 m), crossing the Sidanalm to the gap southeast of the peak, then make the easy ascent to the peak, 2 hrs.; from the peak go across the west ridge, or somewhat south of it, to Nurpensjoch, from which the Halslspitze (2574 m) is easy to reach, cross Nafingalm to Weidener Hütte (Nafinghütte, 1856 m), approx. 2 hrs.

Day 2:
See also adjoining map No. 37 „Ziller Valley Alps – Tux Alps".
a) From Weidener Hütte across Geiseljoch (2292 m), to Geiselalm, 2½ hrs.; from here, cross Nasse Tuxalm, past the Torseen (lakes) to Torjoch (2386 m), 2½ hrs.; descent to Lizumer Hütte (2019 m), ½ hr., total 5½ – 6 hrs.
b) From Weidener Hütte across Grafennsalm to Grafennsjoch (2450 m) north of Hippold-spitze, 3 hrs.; the peak (2642 m) is climbed easily from the west. Climb down over Ausser-lann Hochleger and Niederleger to Innerlannalm and from there up to the magnificent Zir-benweg to Lizumer Hütte (2019 m), approx. 2½ hrs.

Day 3:
From Lizumer Hütte (hut) proceed south, past Junssee (lake), along the scenic high trail to Tuxer-Joch-Haus (hut, 2310 m), 5 – 6 hrs. To continue the hike going west, see adjoining map No. 36 „Innsbruck – Brenner" or make the descent to Hintertux in 2 hours.

Zillertal Alps
Long west-east hike, mainly on Alpine Club trails (also possible in opposite direction).

Day 1:
Ascent to Geraer Hütte (2326 m); from St. Jodok am Brenner (see adjoining map No. 36 „Innsbruck – Brenner") through Valsertal to Gasthof (inn) Touristenrast, 1½ – 2 hrs.; then follow Alpeiner Bach (brook) into the valley (end of the road) and make the steep ascent in hairpin turns to Ochsnerhütte (2081 m), then somewhat less steep across the floors of the Alpeiner Alm to Windschaufelgraben, climb it and follow the hairpin turns to the hut, total approx. 4½ hrs.

Alternatives/Day 1:
Ascent to Tuxer-Joch-Haus (2310 m): a) from St. Jodok through Schmirntal to Kasern, ap-prox. 2½ hrs.; continue to Kaserer Winkl where the road ends, ½ hr., and along the mule track in 2 hrs. to the hut, total approx. 4½ – 5 hrs.; b) less strenuous from Hintertux, 2½ hrs., by taking the Sommerbergalm Chair Lift, ¾ hr.

Day 2:
From the hut, go left of the Alpeiner Ferner (abandoned mine) up to Alpeiner Scharte (2959 m), 2 hrs. Continue the steep climb down to Unterschrammachkar with its small lakes and to Zamser Grund; from there proceed out of the valley to Schlegeis Reservoir (15 min. trail to Dominikushütte, 1805 m, bus-stop), 2 – 2½ hrs.; now follow Berliner Höhenweg (trail) along the lake through Schlegeisgrund to Furtschaglboden and up the tight turns to Furtschaglhaus (2295 m), approx. 2½ hrs., total approx. 7 hrs.

Alternatives/Day 2:
Cross to Spannagelhaus (2531 m), 2 hrs.; then easily over Friesenbergscharte (2910 m) to Friesenberghaus (2498 m) on Friesenbergsee (lake), approx. 3½ hrs.; from here, pro-ceed either directly to Schlegeis Reservoir, 1½ hrs., or take the roundabout way past Olper-erhütte (2388 m), 2 hrs., making the descent to the reservoir in a good hour. Here is the trail to Furtschaglhaus (see above). This route can only be shortened by taking the lifts from Hintertux.

Day 3:
From Furtschaglhaus easily over Schönbichler Horn (3134 m) and its excellent lookout, 2½ – 3 hrs.; go east from the gap, first steep (secured by cables) through the flank onto the back of the ridge, then across it and down an easy trail to the completely dry tongue of the Waxeggkees (glacier); the trail crosses the deep deposits of rock debris at the foot of the Waxegg- and Hornkees (glaciers) and then makes a short climb to Berliner Hütte (2042 m), total 5 – 6 hrs.

Hochfeiler/Gran Pilastro, 3509 m

Day 4:

Past the magnificently situated Schwarzensee (lake) to Rosskar (turnoff on left to Melker-scharte) and along tight turns to Nördliche Mörchenscharte (2957 m), 2½ – 3 hrs.; descent on the other side in steep hairpin turns (secured by cables) to the innermost Floitengrund, which is crossed to pick up on the opposite side of the valley the trail leading to Greizerhütte (2227 m) in about ¾ hr., total 5½ hrs.

Day 5:

Go north across the Griesfeld's slopes, then take the small but tight turns to Lapenscharte (2701 m), 1½ hrs.; descent on the other side under the rocks of the Gigalitz to a morainic ridge and Lapenkar until the fork in the trail; to the right is a lovely high trail (secured by cables) through the cirques of the inner Stillupgrund to Kasseler Hütte (2178 m), total 4½ – 5 hrs.; the trail on the left climbs through Lapenkar past Lapenhütte and makes a steep descent between brooks to Stillupgrund; the trail leads across a bridge to Taxachalm and to Grüne-Wand-Hütte, total 4 – 4½ hrs.

Day 6:

Go through Stillupgrund to the north end of the reservoir, from Kasseler Hütte, approx. 3½ – 4 hrs.; from here, across Krötzelbergalm and Hahnpfalz up to Edelhütte (2238 m), 3 – 3½ hrs.

Day 7:

Past Ahornachalm and Stadelbachalm to Alpengasthof Häusling (1053 m) in Zillergrund, 4 hrs.; go into the valley to Gasthof 'In der Au', 1½ hrs. (taxi sometimes available), and continue on to Bärenbad (inn) in ¾ hr. Shuttle-Bus to Restaurant Adlerblick. Tireless hikers can make the climb over Restaurant Adlerblick and take Dreiländer-Weg along the Zillergründl Reservoir to Plauener Hütte (2364 m), 2½ hrs.; from here the tour can be set forth past Richterhütte (2367 m) and further north past Zittauer Hütte to Gerlos or east by way of Krimmler Tauernhaus (1631 m) to the Venediger Group (see adjoining map No. 38 „Venediger Group – Oberpinzgau").

Alpine Inns and Huts

All information without guarantee. Please request opening times before starting out of town and ask if overnight guests are welcome!

Telephone numbers of the most important small restaurants and inns with sleeping accommodations are given on page 76.

Tux Alps (Tuxer Alpen)

Astegg, 1176 m (D 2), private inn, mailing address: 6292 Finkenberg, open all year. Access: from Finkenberg, 1 hr.; from Mayrhofen, 2 hrs. Crossing: to Penkenhaus, 1½ hrs.; to Gschößwandhaus, 2 hrs.

Bergrast, 1794 m (D 2), inn on Gschößberg, see Gschößwandhaus.

Eggalm, 1948 m (B 3), private restaurant, mailing address: 6293 Lanersbach, open all year. Access: from Lanersbach, 2¼ hrs. or by gondola lift. Crossing: to Lizumer Hütte, 4 hrs. Peak: Grüblspitze, 2395 m, 1 hr. (easy).

Gschößwandhaus, 1762 m (D 2), mountain station of Penken Cable Car, private, mailing address: 6290 Mayrhofen, open all year. Access: from Finkenberg, approx. 3 hrs.; from Mayrhofen, 3 – 3½ hrs. Crossing: to Penkenjochhaus over Gschößberg, 1¼ hrs.; to Penkenhaus, 1¼ hrs.; to Mösl-Gasthaus, 1½ hrs. Peak: Gschößberg, 2005 m, ½ hr.

Lizumer Hütte, 2019 m (A 2), Alpine Club, mailing address: 6112 Wattens, open summer and winter. Access: from Wattens, 5 hrs.; from Walchen (available by car), 2 hrs. Crossings: to Lanersbach, 3½ hrs.; to Weidener Hütte over Krovenzjoch, 5 hrs.; to Tuxer-Joch-Haus, 6 hrs. Peaks: Mölser Sonnenspitze, 2427 m, 2 hrs. (easy); Geier, 2857 m, 3 hrs. (easy); Lizumer Reckner, 2886 m, 3½ hrs. (only for experienced climbers).

Penkenhaus, 1814 m (D 2), private, mailing address: 6292 Finkenberg, open all year. Access: from Mayrhofen, 3¾ hrs.; from Finkenberg by way of Astegg, 2½ – 3 hrs.; from mountain station of Penken Cable Car, 1¼ hrs. Crossing: to Penkenjochhaus, ¾ hr.

Penkenjochhaus, 2095 m (D 2), private, mailing address: 6292 Finkenberg, open all year. Access: from Finkenberg by way of Penkenhaus, 3½ hrs.; from Mayrhofen, 4 – 4½ hrs.; from mountain station of Penken Cable Car, 1¼ hrs. Crossings: to Vorderlanersbach over Schrofenalm, 2½ hrs.; to Rastkogelhütte over Rastkogel, approx. 4 hrs. Peaks: Wanglspitz, 2420 m, 1½ hrs. (easy); Rastkogel, 2762 m, 3 hrs. (easy).

Perler, 1130 m (D 1), private inn, mailing address: 6283 Hippach, open all year. Access: from Hippach, 1½ hrs.; available by car. Crossing: to Rastkogelhütte, 3 hrs.

Zillertal Alps

(Tuxer Hauptkamm, Zillertaler Hauptkamm and Reichenspitz Group)

Adlerblick, 1900 m (I 16), private restaurant, mailing address: 6290 Mayrhofen, open in summer. Access: by car or bus to Bärenbad; then either walk 45 min. or take the shuttle bus. Nearby is the new High-Alpine Chapel (Hochgebirgskapelle).

Alpenrose, 1398 m (E 3, F 15), private, mailing address: 6290 Mayrhofen, open in summer. Access: from Mayrhofen, 2 – 2½ hrs. Crossing: to Edelhütte, 2½ hrs.

Alpenrosehütte, 1873 m (D 8), private, mailing address: 6295 Ginzling, open in summer. Access: from Ginzling, 4½ hrs.; from Breitlahner (inn), bus stop, 2½ hrs. Crossings: to Berliner Hütte, ½ hr.; to Furtschaglhaus, 6 hrs.

Bärenbad, 1450 m (I 16), private, mailing address: 6290 Mayrhofen, open in summer. Access: from Mayrhofen, 4¾ hrs.; also accessible by car (toll road! Toll road closes when carpark is full) or bus. Crossing: to Plauener Hütte, 2 hrs.

Berliner Hütte, 2042 m (D 8), Alpine Club, mailing address: 6295 Ginzling, open in summer. Access: from Ginzling, 4½ – 5 hrs.; from Breitlahner (inn), bus stop, approx. 3 hrs. Crossings: to Alpenrosehütte, 20 min.; to Greizerhütte over Nördliche Mörchenscharte, 5½ – 6 hrs.; to Furtschaglhaus over Schönbichler Horn, 6 hrs.; into Gunggl over Melkerscharte, 6 – 7 hrs. Peak: Schönbichler Horn, 3134 m, 4 hrs. Numerous high tours of varying difficulty.

Brandberger Kolmhaus, 1845 m (G 14), private, mailing address: 6290 Mayrhofen, open in summer. Access: from Brandberg, approx. 2 hrs.; from Mayrhofen, 3½ – 4 hrs. Crossings: to Gasthof Kühle Rast (bus stop) over Brandberger Joch, 3½ hrs.; to Gerlosstein-Berghotel (inn), approx. 2½ hrs. Peaks: Brandberger Kolm, 2700 m, 2½ – 3 hrs. (medium); Torhelm, 2452 m, 2 hrs. (easy).

Breitlahner, 1256 m (C 6), private inn, mailing address: 6295 Ginzling, open in summer. Access: from Ginzling, 2 hrs.; by car or bus to hut. Crossings: to Berliner Hütte, 3 hrs.; to Dominikushütte, 2 hrs.; to Friesenberghaus, 4 hrs.

Dominikushütte, 1805 m (B 7), private, mailing address: 6295 Ginzling, open in summer. Access: by car (toll road) or bus to hut; from Ginzling, 4½ hrs.; from Breitlahner, 2 hrs. Crossings: to Pfitscher-Joch-Haus (South Tyrol), 2 hrs.; to Friesenberghaus, 2½ hrs.; to Olpererhütte, 2 hrs.; to Furtschaglhaus, 2½ hrs. Peak: Olperer, 3476 m, 5 hrs. (only for experienced climbers).

Edelhütte, 2238 m (E 4, F 16), Alpine Club, mailing address: 6290 Mayrhofen, open in summer. Access: from Mayrhofen, 4½ – 5 hrs.; from Ahorn Cable Car mountain station, 1 hr. Crossing: to Stilluphaus in Stillupgrund, 2½ hrs. Peak: Ahornspitze, 2973 m, 2 – 2½ hrs. (only for experienced climbers).

Finkau, 1420 m (K 13), private inn, mailing address: 5743 Krimml, open all year. Access: by car to Gasthaus (inn); from Gerlos Pass, 2 hrs.; from Gerlos, 3 hrs. Crossing: to Zittauer Hütte, 3 hrs.

Gabler, 3263 m, and/und/e Reichenspitze, 3303 m

Friesenberghaus, 2498 m (B 6), Alpine Club, mailing address: 6295 Ginzling, open in summer. Access: from Breitlahner, 3½ hrs.; from Dominikushütte, 2 hrs. Crossings: to Spannagelhaus over Friesenbergscharte, 3 hrs.; to Olpererhütte, 2 hrs. Peaks: Hoher Riffler, 3231 m, 2 hrs., only vague trail (only for experienced climbers); Petersköpfl, 2679 m, ¾ hr. (easy).

Furtschaglhaus, 2295 m (C 9), Alpine Club, mailing address: 6295 Ginzling, open in summer. Access: from Dominikushütte, 2½ hrs. Crossing: to Berliner Hütte by way of Schönbichler Horn, 6½ hrs. Peak: Schönbichler Horn, 3134 m, 2½ hrs. (medium). Many high Alpine tours of varying difficulty.

Gamshütte, 1921 m (D 4), Alpine Club, mailing address: 6290 Mayrhofen, open in summer. Access: from Finkenberg, 3 hrs.; from Ginzling, 3 hrs. Peaks: Grinbergspitzen, 2884 m, 2765 m and 2867 m, approx. 2½ hrs. (medium).

Geraer Hütte, 2324 m (A 7), Alpine Club, mailing address: 6154 St. Jodok am Brenner, open in summer. Access: from St. Jodok, 4½ hrs.; by car or bus to Touristenrast (inn), from there 2½ hrs. Crossings: to Olpererhütte, 4 hrs.; to Schmirn over Wildlahnerweg, 2½ hrs.; to Tuxer-Joch-Haus over Kleegrubenscharte, 4 – 4½ hrs.

Gerlosstein-Berghotel, 1620 m (G 13), private, mailing address: 6280 Hainzenberg, open all year. Access: near Gerlos Cable Car mountain station; from Hainzenberg, Ötschenwirt bus stop, 2 hrs.; from Zell am Ziller, 3½ hrs.; from Ramsberg, 2½ – 3 hrs. Crossings: to Mayrhofen, 3 hrs.; to Brandberger Kolmhaus, 2½ – 3 hrs. Peaks: Gerlossteinwand, 2166 m, 1½ hrs. (easy); Hochfeld, 2350 m, 2 hrs. (easy).

Grawandhütte, 1636 m (C 8), private, mailing address: 6295 Ginzling, open in summer. Access: from Breitlahner, 1½ hrs. Crossing: to Alpenrosehütte, ¾ hr.

Greizerhütte, 2227 m (E 7, F 19), Alpine Club, mailing address: 6290 Mayrhofen, open in summer. Access: from Ginzling, approx. 4 hrs. Crossings: to Berliner Hütte over Nördliche Mörchenscharte, 5½ hrs.; to Grüne-Wand-Hütte over Lapenscharte, 4 hrs.; to Kasseler Hütte, 5 hrs. Peaks: Grosser Löffler, 3378 m, 3½ hrs. (medium); Schwarzenstein, 3369 m, 4 hrs. (medium).

Grüne-Wand-Hütte, 1436 m (G 18), private, mailing address: 6290 Mayrhofen, open in summer. Access: from Mayrhofen, 4 hrs. or taxi from „Europahaus" in Mayrhofen; from Alpengasthof Wasserfall, 2 Std. Crossings: to Kasseler Hütte, 2 hrs.; to Greizerhütte over Lapenscharte, 6 hrs.

Häusling, 1053 m (GH 15), private inn, mailing address: 6290 Mayrhofen, open all year. Access: from Mayrhofen, 2½ hrs.; also accessible by car (toll road! Toll road closes when carpark is full) or bus. Crossing: to Gasthof In der Au, 1½ hrs.; also by car or bus.

Hochferner-Biwak (Günther-Messner-Bivouac), 2429 m (B 9), Alpine Club, open all year. Access: from St. Jakob in Pfitsch, 4 hrs.; von Stein, 3 hrs.; from 5th curve on Pfitscher-Joch-Strasse, 1 hr.

Höllensteinhütte, 1710 m (B 4), private, mailing address: 6293 Lanersbach, open in summer. Access: from the bus stop at Juns (approx. 2 km south of Lanersbach), 1½ hrs.

In der Au, 1265 m (H 16), private inn, mailing address: 6290 Mayrhofen, open all year. Access: from Mayrhofen, 4 hrs.; also accessible by car (toll road! Toll road closes when carpark is full) or bus. Crossing: to Bärenbad, ¾ hr.

Innerböden, 1301 m (D 5), private inn, mailing address: 6295 Ginzling, open all year. Access: from Ginzling, 1 hr.

Kasseler Hütte, 2178 m (G 18), Alpine Club, mailing address: 6290 Mayrhofen, open in summer. Access: from Mayrhofen, approx. 6 hrs.; from Grüne-Wand-Hütte, 2 hrs. (accessible by taxi from „Europahaus" in Mayrhofen). Crossings: high trail over Lapenscharte to Greizerhütte, 4 – 5 hrs.; to Edelhütte on Siebenschneidsteig, 9 – 10 hrs. Peaks: Grüne-Wand-Spitze, 2946 m, 2½ hrs.; Wollbachspitze, 3209 m, 3 hrs.

Klaushof, 1022 m (G 15), private inn, mailing address: 6290 Mayrhofen, open all year. Access: from Mayrhofen, 2 hrs.; also accessible by car (toll road! Toll road closes when carpark is full) or bus. Crossing: to Häusling, ½ hr.

Lacknerbrunn, 1006 m (D 3), private inn, mailing address: 6290 Mayrhofen, open all year. Access: from Mayrhofen, 1½ hrs.; by car (toll road) or taxi from „Europahaus" in Mayrhofen. Crossings: to Alpengasthof Wasserfall, ¾ hr.; to Edelhütte, 4 hrs.

Max-Hütte, 1445 m (D 6), private, mailing: 6292 Finkenberg, open in summer. Access: from Ginzling, 1½ hrs. Crossing: to Berliner Hütte over Melkerscharte, 7 hrs.

Olpererhütte, 2388 m (B 7), Alpine Club, mailing address: 6295 Ginzling, open in summer. Access: from Schlegeis Reservoir (accessible by car/toll road or bus), 1½ Std. Crossings: to Friesenberghaus, 2 hrs.; to Geraer Hütte over Alpeiner Scharte, 4 hrs. Peaks: Olperer, 3476 m, 3 hrs. (only for experienced climbers); Gefrorene-Wand-Spitzen, 3288 m, 3½ hrs. (for experienced climbers).

Pfitscher-Joch-Haus (Rif. Passo di Vizze), 2275 m (A 9), private, mailing address: 39040 St. Jakob in Pfitsch, open in summer. Access: from Stein, 2½ hrs.; from St. Jakob, 1¾ Std.; from Schlegeis Reservoir, 2 hrs. Crossings: to Landshuter Europahütte, 3½ hrs.; to Geraer Hütte, 5 hrs.; to Furtschaglhaus, 5 hrs. Peaks: Schrammacher, 3410 m, 4 hrs. (only for experienced climbers); Hohe Wand-Spitze, 3289 m, 4 hrs. (difficult).

Plauener Hütte, 2364 m (K 16), Alpine Club, mailing address: 6283 Hippach, open in summer. Access: from Mayrhofen, 7½ – 8 hrs.; by car (toll road! Toll road closes when carpark is full) or bus to Bärenbad, from there 2 hrs. Crossing: to Richterhütte over Gamsscharte, 3 hrs. Peak: Richterspitze, 3052 m, 2½ hrs. (medium).

Richterhütte, 2367 m (K 16), Alpine Club, mailing address: 5743 Krimml, open in summer. Access: from Krimmler Tauernhaus, 2½ hrs.; from Krimml, 5 – 6 hrs. Crossings: to Plauener Hütte, 3 hrs.; to Zittauer Hütte, 3½ hrs.; to Birnlückenhütte, 7¼ hrs. Peaks: Windbachtalkogel, 2843 m, 1½ hrs. (easy); Richterspitze, 3052 m, 2½ hrs. (medium).

Rosshag, 1096 m (C 6), private inn, mailing address: 6295 Ginzling, open all year. Access: from Ginzling, approx. 1 hr., or by car. Crossing: to Breitlahner, 1 hr., or by car.

Schwarzensteinhütte (Rifugio Vittorio Veneto), 2922 m (E 8), Italian Alpine Club, mailing address: 39030 Luttach, open in summer. Access: from Luttach, 5½ hrs. Peak: Schwarzenstein, 3396 m, 1½ hrs. (medium).

Spannagelhaus, 2531 m (A 6), Austrian Tourist Club, mailing address: 6294 Hintertux, open in summer and winter. A few minutes from the hut is Spannagel Cave! Access: from Hintertux, 3½ hrs., or by cable car. Crossings: to Tuxer-Joch-Haus, 1½ hrs.; to Friesenberghaus over Friesenbergscharte, approx. 3½ hrs. In der Nähe der Hütte befindet sich ein Klettergarten. Erfahrene Bergführer lehren Sie die Grundbegriffe des Bergsteigens wie Trittsicherheit, Seiltechnik, richtiges Klettern usw.

Stein, 1555 m (A 10), private inn, mailing address I-39040 St. Jakob in Pfitsch, open all year. Access: from St. Jakob in Pfitsch, 1 hr., or by car. Crossing: to Landshuter Europahütte across Pfitscher Joch, 4¾ hrs.

Steinerkogl, 1270 m (E 2, F 14), private inn, mailing address: 6290 Mayrhofen, open in summer. Access: from Mayrhofen, 1½ hrs.; from Brandberg, ¾ hrs. Crossings: to Brandberger Kolmhaus, 2 hrs.; to Gerlosstein-Berghotel, 2½ hrs.

Stilluphaus, 1192 m (FG 17), private inn, mailing address: 6290 Mayrhofen, open in summer. Access: from Mayrhofen, 3 hrs. or taxi from „Europahaus" in Mayrhofen; from Alpengasthof Wasserfall, 1 Std. Crossing: to Grüne-Wand-Hütte, 1 hr.

Tuxer-Joch-Haus, 2310 m (A 5), Austrian Tourist Club, mailing address A6294 Hintertux, open in summer. Access: from Hintertux, 2½ hrs.; from Sommerbergalm mountain station, ¾ hr.; from Kasern im Schmirntal, 2 hrs. Crossings: to Spannagelhaus, 2 hrs.; to Geraer Hütte over Kleegrubenscharte, 4½ hrs. Peaks: Hornspitze, 2650 m, 1½ hrs. (only for experienced climbers); Frauenwand, 2541 m, 1 hr. (easy).

Wasserfall, 1120 m (E 4, F 16), in the Stillupgrund, private inn, mailing address: 6290 Mayrhofen, open in summer. Access: from Mayrhofen, 2 hrs.; accessible by car (toll road) or taxi from „Europahaus" in Mayrhofen. Crossing: by way of Stilluphaus to Grüne-Wand-Hütte, 2 hrs.

Wiesenhof, 1058 m (E 3, F 15), private inn, mailing address: 6290 Mayrhofen, open all year. Access: from Mayrhofen, 1½ hrs.; cars allowed to hut.

Zittauer Hütte, 2328 m (K 14), Alpine club, mailing address: 5743 Krimml, open in summer. Access: from Finkau-Gasthaus (inn), 3 hrs.; from Gerlos, 5 hrs.; from Gerlos-Pass, 5 hrs. Crossing: to Richterhütte, 3½ hrs. Peaks: Rosskopf, 2845 m, 1 – 1½ hrs. (easy); Reichenspitze, 3303 m, 4 hrs. (difficult).

Our thanks to the tourist offices and Alpine Clubs who helped us update this KOMPASS Guide and who made photo material available to us.

Towns

Telephone and fax numbers of tourist offices and town halls are given on page 77.

Steinmandl in the environmentally protected Naturpark Zillertaler Alpen
Steinmandl im Naturpark Zillertaler Alpen
Ometti di pietre nel parco naturale Zillertaler Alpen

BRANDBERG E 2/F 14

Township, Schwaz County, Population: 350, Elevation: 1082 m, Postal Code: 6290 Brandberg. **Information:** Brandberg Town Hall. **Railroad Station:** Mayrhofen (6 km). **Bus service:** from Mayrhofen.

High on a mountainside overlooking the Ziller Valley is the small resort town Brandberg. In the early 19th century Mayrhofen became independent of the former 'Pramberg Township', leaving Brandberg an authentic Alpine farm community, with its hamlets, lone farms and summer pastures strewn along the sunny slope of the 'Pram' or 'Brandberg' and down the lengthy Ziller river valley. Over the years many people have foresaken the rugged hillside life here. In recent years Brandberg has become a popular tourism town.

Brandberg, has an area of 156 km² and is one of the largest towns by size in the Ziller Valley. It has an agreeable climate and is an ideal place to start many hikes. Nature lovers will enjoy the large variety of untouched, pristine countryside as well as cultivated landscape. The town is accessed by a good road; ample parking available in town.

Attractions in Town and Nearby

The neo-Classical **Parish Church of the Holy Cross** contains a remarkable late Gothic Madonna at the side altar; on the outside of the church is a war memorial. „Mater dolorosa" above the door; mosaics. The new cemetery chapel dates from 1977/78. – The **village**

39

fountain with a small carving by Albin Moroder of Mayrhofen, who also executed the **Stations of the Cross** on the way to Brandberg Chapel. – The **main ridge of the Ziller Valley Alps is an environmentally protected area.**

Walks and Hikes

To Berggasthaus Steinerkogl (inn, 1270 m) via Emberg, ¾ hr. – To Brandberger Kolmhaus (hut, 1845 m), approx. 2 hrs. and to Brandberger Kolm (2700 m, peak), total approx. 4½ hrs. – To Gerlosstein-Berghotel (inn, 1620 m), by way of Laberg- and Kotahornalm, 3½ hrs. – Deep into the Ziller Valley (Zillergrund) to Gasthaus Klaushof (snacks, 1022 m), approx. 1 hr., to Häusling (inn, 1253 m) total approx. 1½ hrs., to In der Au (inn, 1265 m) total 3 hrs., to Bärenbad (inn, 1450 m), total 4 hrs. This toll road can be traveled either in your own car (toll road is closed for cars when parking is full) or by public bus. – From Bärenbad to Zillergründl Reservoir, approx. 1 – 1½ hrs. – To Plauener Hütte (hut, 2364 m) from Bärenbad, approx. 2 hrs. – To restaurant Adlerblick (1900 m), 45 min. from Bärenbad or by shuttle-bus. – To Kainzenhüttenalm (1550 m) in Sundergrund, from In der Au approx. 1½ hrs. – To Bodenalm (1670 m) from Häusling, approx. 1½ hrs.

FINKENBERG D 3

Township, Schwaz County, Population: 1520, Elevation: 839 m, Postal Code: 6292. **Information:** Finkenberg – Tux Tourism Association. **Railroad Station:** Mayrhofen (3 km). **Bus service:** to and from Mayrhofen and the bottom station of the Hintertuxer Gletscherbahnen (lifts) in Hintertux. **Cable Lifts:** Finkenberger Almbahnen Double Chair Lift, various chairlifts and towlifts at Penkenjoch.

A popular year-round resort, Finkenberg stretches the length of a sunny terrace high above the deep gorge at the mouth of the Tuxbach. Finkenberg is the Ziller Valley's second largest town by surface area, although more than half of its land is wasteland. Some parts of Finkenberg and several of the farms located on the south side of outer Tux Valley at elevations of up to 1400 m were first documented as far back as the 14th century. The town also includes dairy pastures at even higher elevations and spreads along the west bank of the Zemmbach all the way to the head of the Zamsergrund and Schlegeisgrund, right up to the present Austrian-Italian border.

In 1991 the Tyrolean State Government declared this unique Alpine landscape („Ruhegebiet Zillertaler Hauptkamm", now „Naturpark Zillertaler Alpen") an environmentally protected area, meaning that no ski lifts or public roads will be erected here in future.

Finkenberg became world-famous in 1980, when the town's favorite son, Leonhard Stock, won an Olympic gold medal in the men's downhill skiing event and thus also the World Champion title.

Attractions in Town and Nearby

St. Leonhard Parish Church, erected 1720, enlarged in the 19th century; interior primarily original. – **Teufelsbrücke** (Devil's Bridge) over the deep Tuxbach gorge is a timber construction dating from 1876. – Small **waterfall** above town. – **Nature trail „Glocke".** – **Moor nature trail** on **Penkenjoch.**

Walks and Hikes

From the church by way of Sporer, the waterfall, forest trail and back, 1 hr. – To Stein (Gasthof/inn Gletscherblick), ascent from the church and descent via Persal to Teufelsbrücke, return from there through the gorge (Klammweg), 2 hrs. – Circular walk from the church, across Teufelsbrücke to Gasthof Schöne Aussicht (inn), continue along the reservoir, to Martins Wirtshaus (inn) and to Jochberg, along the road past Pension Forellenhof to Pension Hochsteg, return from there along the rim of the gorge, cross Teufelsbrücke into town, total approx. 2½ hrs. – To Gasthof Astegg (inn, 1176 m) via Stein, 1 hr.; descent toward Mayrhofen on Mariensteig, turning off west of Zemmbach onto the meadow path that leads back to Finkenberg, approx. 2 hrs. – To Innerberg (bus stop) on the road through Persal, ¾ hr.; across Rosengartenbrücke to Gschwendt and Brunnhaus and back over

Teufelsbrücke or across the footbridge and past the swimming pool to the road near Persal, 2 ½ – 3 hrs. – To Vorderlanersbach by way of Altenstall – Katzenmoos – Möser – Ausserrettenbach, 3 hrs. – To Gschößwandhaus (1762 m) via Gasthof Astegg (inn), 3 hrs. – To Penkenhaus (1814 m), 3 hrs.; further, to Penkenjochhaus (2095 m), mountain station of the Finkenberger Alm Cable Lift, ¾ hr. – To Gamshütte (1921 m) along Hermann-Hecht-Weg, 3 hrs. – To Gasthof Innerböden (inn, 1301 m) and Oberbödenalm (1500 m), from Ginzling, 2 hrs. – To Max-Hütte (1445 m), from Ginzling, 1½ hrs. – To Greizerhütte (2227 m), from Ginzling through Floitengrund, approx. 3 ¼ hrs. – To Gasthaus (inn) Breitlahner (1256 m), from Ginzling, 1½ – 2 hrs. – To Berliner Hütte (2042 m), from Gasthaus (inn) Breitlahner through Zemmgrund, via Grawand- and Alpenrosehütte (huts), 2 ½ hrs. – To Dominikushütte (1805 m), from Ginzling, 4½ hrs. – To Furtschaglhaus (2295 m), from Dominikushütte via Zamsgatterl and Berliner Höhenweg, along Schlegeis Reservoir to the hut, 3 hrs. – To Pfitscher-Joch-Haus (2275 m), from Dominikushütte via Zamsgatterl and in Zamser Grund up to Pfitscher Joch, 2 hrs. – To Olpererhütte (2388 m), from Dominikushütte, first approx. 10 min. along the reservoir to the turnoff (trail No. 502) to the right to the hut, 1 hr. – To Friesenberghaus (2498 m), first to Olpererhütte and from there along Berliner Höhenweg (trail No. 526), past Friesenbergsee (lake) to the hut, 3 hrs. or from the reservoir directly to the hut (trail No. 532), 2 hrs.

GERLOS

Township, Schwaz County, Population: 800, Elevation: 1245 m, Postal Code: 6281. **Information:** Gerlos – Zell Tourism Association. **Railroad Station:** Zell am Ziller (18 km). **Bus service:** from Zell am Ziller, Mayrhofen and Wald im Pinzgau. **Cable Lifts:** Several chairlifts and towlifts.

With the improved federal highway over Gerlos Pass (1531 m), construction of Durlassboden Reservoir and the creation of ski resorts and modern recreational facilities, the technological age has made its way to the remote heights of Gerlos Valley. But just off the road are peaceful Alpine pastures and out-of-the-way mountain peaks of all difficulties, not to mention the friendly, rambling community where everyone is made to feel at home.

Attractions in Town and Nearby
Parish church of Sts. Leonard and Lampert was erected 1730 – 1735 by Hans Holzmeister from Hippach; ceiling paintings by Josef Michael Schmutzer from Wessobrunn; original altars partially renovated; madonna by Josef Bachlechner, 1911, at the main altar. – **Durlassboden Reservoir** at the junction of the Wildgerlos Valley and the main Gerlos Valley.

Walks and Hikes
Into Schönachtal to Stinkmossalm (1348 m), approx. ¾ hr., continue in a slow climb to the Jausenstation Lackenalm (snacks, 1400 m), ½ hr. – To Issalm through Schönachtal and past Pasteinalm (1692 m) deep into the valley basin, approx. 3 hrs. – To Gmünd via Gerlostalalm (1756 m) and back along the forest trail, approx. 4 hrs. – Into Wimmertal to Grundhütte (1685 m); from Gmünd, approx. 1½ – 2 hrs. – Up to Gerlos Pass (1531 m) via Zentralpenweg (Variante) 02 and the Königsleitenalmen, 4 hrs. – Up to Schönbichl (2049 m), from Gerlos past Kreidlschlagalm onto the broad ridge that is the northern end of the Schönachkamm; along the ridge to the grassy summit with its excellent view, approx. 2½ hrs. – Up to Arbiskogel (2048 m), go south straight out of Gerlos, 2 – 2½ hrs. (take the Fürstalm Lift to Fürstalm, 1824 m, to shorten the hiking time by 1½ hrs.); crossing to Kirchspitze (2312 m), ¾ hrs. (easy); descent possible via Kothüttenalm to Gmünd. – To Brandberger Kolmhaus (1845 m) from Gasthof Kühle Rast (bus stop) over Brandberger Joch (2037 m) approx. 4 hrs. – Up to Isskogel (2268 m) via Ebenfeldaste (1864 m), when using Isskogel Lift., 1½ hrs. – To Zittauer Hütte (2328 m) through Wildgerlos Valley; from Gerlos 6 hrs., from Finkau (inn), 3 hrs.

GERLOSBERG   G 12

Township, Schwaz County, Population: 460, Elevation: 1100 m, Postal Code: 6280. **Information:** Gerlos – Zell Tourism Association. **Railroad Station:** Zell am Ziller (5 km). **Bus service:** from Zell am Ziller.

This small town was originally a township belonging to Salzburg court in Zell am Ziller and in many ways still enjoys close ties to the valley's main town. For further information see Zell am Ziller.

HAINZENBERG   F 12

Township, Schwaz County, Population: 670, Elevation: 944 m, Postal Code: 6280. **Information:** Hainzenberg Town Hall. **Railroad Station:** Zell am Ziller (5 km). **Bus service:** from Zell am Ziller, Mayrhofen, Gerlos – Wald im Pinzgau. **Cable Lifts:** Gerlosstein Cable Car, Arbiskögerl Towlift and Chair Lift.

At the foot of the mighty Gerlosstein lies the town of Hainzenberg, which borders to the south on Ramsau im Zillertal, to the east on Gerlos, to the north to Gerlosberg and to the northwest on Zell am Ziller. The town consists largely of scattered groups of dwellings. The actual heart of town is in Hainzenberg with its town hall, primary school, and kindergarten as well as the bottom station of the Gerlosstein Cable Car. Hainzenberg mountain was the scene of gold mining activity from the early 16th century until the 19th century. For more information, visit the Demonstration Gold Mine (Goldschaubergwerk). Today, the town relies on agriculture and tourism for its livelihood. Comfortable inns and B&Bs are also available. Improvement of the federal highway also benefited the area (circular tours of Zell am See, Lofer, Wörgl, Krimmler Waterfalls, Pass Thurn and Kitzbühel).

Attractions in Town and Nearby

The **Mining Chapel** (Bergwerkkapelle) on view in **Haus Unterflörler** (erected 1250) is a national landmark for its art-history importance. The **Mining Chapel** is tended by Walter Burgstaller, a professional woodcarver and mineral collector, and contains an extensive **mineral collection.** – Watch cheese being made at the „**Schaukäserei**"; together with an information stand and a small zoo, this is a favorite place for excursions. – This is also the starting point for visits to the **Demonstration Gold Mine** (Goldschaubergwerk). Take the one-hour guided tour to learn all about the underground working conditions, and how the miners lived. – **Maria Rast Pilgrimage Chapel** (Wallfahrtskapelle Maria Rast), whose predecessor was the Unterflörler Chapel, is very worthwhile; late Gothic portal and four late Gothic windows (now restored); 18th-century furnishings; stuccowork and good ceiling paintings by Josef Michael Schmutzer from Wessobrunn, 1741; lovely Rococo main altar by Stefan Föger, 1748, with Baroque madonna; pulpit also by Föger (?).

Walks and Hikes

To Zell am Ziller over Maria Rast on the forest trail, 1 hr. – To Gerlosstein-Berghotel (1620 m) from the last hairpin turn on the federal road, 2½ hrs., or 2 hrs. from Ötschenwirt. Gerlosstein-Berghotel can also be reached by the Gerlosstein Cable Car.

HIPPACH   F 12-13

Township, Schwaz County, Population: 1380, Elevation: 608 m, Postal Code: 6283. **Information:** Hippach – Ramsau – Schwendau Tourism Association. **Railroad Station:** Ramsau-Hippach. **Bus service:** from Jenbach, Mayrhofen, Gerlos – Wald im Pinzgau. **Cable Lifts:** see Mayrhofen.

The stately town of Hippach is at the hub of the communities fanning out at the foot of the densely populated Schwendberg on the west side of the upper Ziller Valley. Although Hippach was first officially mentioned in the mid 13th century, the town was settled and the church erected at a much earlier date. The name „Hippach" is of Germanic origin and denotes the town's location on the bank of the now tamed river, which formerly washed up the easily recognizable fan of debris between Hippach and Schwendau. At the end of the 17th century, a spring with medicinal properties brought Hippach the reputation of a „bath".

Hippach's development to a modern recreational center is owed to its sunny location and good accessibility, to its warm hospitality and, not least of all, to a long list of talented and original inhabitants including singers, artists, teachers and well-known celebrities.

Attractions in Town and Nearby

The originally Gothic **Church of Sts. Ingenuin and Albin** was renovated and adapted to the Baroque style following an earthquake in 1699. Its Gothic remnants include the portal transferred to the east transept and the tower on the south side; late 17th-century stuccowork; central ceiling paintings from late 19th century; frescoes on the sides by Josef Michael Schmutzer from Wessobrunn, 1746; to the side, a painting by the local artist Matthäus Schiestl, 1914, who with Johann Sporer executed the statues at the side altars; Baroque stat-ues at the main altar. – Especially recommended is a drive along the heights of the **Zillertaler Höhenstrasse**, a good place to start many interesting hikes. – Three **linden trees** declared natural monuments. – Worthwhile in **Laimach** is a visit to the **Museum „Strasser Häusl,"** where the Strasser family once lived and popularized the hymn „Silent Night, Holy Night" throughout the world.

Walks and Hikes

To Mayrhofen, either by crossing the Ziller Bridge and following the east bank, or by going west via Stockach, Mühlbach and Burgstallschrofen, approx. 1 hr. – To Zell am Ziller along the Ziller-Promenade on the east bank or along the road through Laimach – Zellbergeben, approx. 1 hr. – To the Laimacher and Talbach waterfalls along Prof.-Dr.-Rieser-Weg. The turnoff to the waterfalls is marked at the bend in the road; return by Laimach, approx. 2 hrs. – To the Keiler Waterfall and back via Schwendau, approx. 2 hrs. – To Gasthof Mösl, 2½ hrs. – To Gschößwandhaus (1762 m), from Gasthof Mösl, 1½ hrs. – To Rastkogelhütte (2117 m), from Gasthof Mösl, 2 hrs.

MAYRHOFEN   E 2/F 14

Market Township, Schwaz County, Population: 3980, Elevation: 633 m, Postal Code: 6290. **Information:** Mayrhofen Tourism Association. **Railroad Station:** Mayrhofen. **Bus service:** to and from Jenbach, the bottom station of the Hintertuxer Gletscherbahnen (lifts) in Hintertux, Brandberg, Ginzling, Gerlos – Wald in Pinzgau, to the Bergrestaurant Schlegeis at the Schlegeis Reservoir, Gasthof Wasserfall (inn) at the Stillup Reservoir, Gasthof Bärenbad and the Zillergründl Reservoir. In winter free ski bus service to the lifts. **Cable Lifts:** Cable cars, chairlifts and towlifts.

Alpine pasture on Penken/Alm am Penken/Alpeggio al Penken

Mayrhofen is Tyrol's oldest tourism center. This holiday town is located in a valley basin at the rear of the Ziller Valley, against the imposing mountain backdrop of the Nature Park Zillertal Alps.

Until 1801 Mayrhofen was part of Brandberg Municipality. The town, once a small farming town, was accessible only over mountain trails from the south and a poor road along the valley floor from the north.

Nowadays, there's something for everyone in Mayrhofen. Although the town is now the tourism center of the Ziller Valley and has undergone vast development and modernization, it still retains the charm of a small village.

Attractions in Town and Nearby

Old **farmhouses** can be admired in the neighborhood Haus and in Brandberg, for example the 400-year old farmhouse „zum Griena," that is an old-fashioned inn today, and Gratzerhaus from the second half of the 17th century. Lovers of modern art will be fascinated by Karg Haus on Scheulingstrasse, whose facade was decorated by the Tyrolean artist Patrizia

Karg. – The **Parish Church of Our Lady** in Mayrhofen with its ceiling painting „The Rose of Jericho" by Max Weiler is also noteworthy for art lovers. – Get to know everything about cheese, life on the alm and local traditions at the **Erlebnis Sennerei Zillertal dairy**. Since 2000 visitors are shown how milk and cheese are made here at the 6,000-m² dairy. – The **large relief of the Zillertal Alps** at the **Europahaus** not only gives you a good impression of the local mountains with the unique Nature Park Zillertal Alps, but also is a good place to plan hikes and mountain tours. – **Naturpark** (Nature Park) **Zillertaler Alpen**, an **environmentally protected area**.

View to/Blick auf/Veduta di Mayrhofen

Walks and Hikes

To the prilgrimage chapel at Burgschrofen from the lower town square (Unterer Dorfplatz), ½ hr. – To Ramsau through Durst, then following the forest past Laubichl, Hollenzen and Eckartau, 1 hr. – To Zimmereben, after a 20 min. climb the trail turns north from Mariensteig, from the lower town square (Unterer Dorfplatz), approx. 1 hr. – To Gasthof Zillergründl along the unpaved road, ½ hr.; return over the trail that turns left at the bridge, past Kumbichl, ¾ hr. – To Edelhütte (2238 m) either with Ahornbahn (lift) to Hahnpfalz and one hour to the hut or from Mayrhofen over Gasthaus (inn) Alpenrose and Fellenbergalm, approx. 4½ – 5 Std. – To Brandberg Pilgrimage Chapel through Scheulingwald (forest), ¾ hr. – From here make a right turn to Brandberg on the unpaved road, ¾ hr. – To Zell am Ziller on the east bank's Ziller-Promenade, 2 hrs. – To Gasthof (inn) Astegg by way of Marienstein, approx. 2 hrs. – From there, descent to Finkenberg, ¾ hr., and return through the meadows, about 1 hr. – To Gasthof Lacknerbrunn (1006 m) above the hamlet Haus, to the hamlet Schmelzhütten with Mayrhofen Power Plant, where the romantic trail sets out through the gorge (Stillupklamm) that runs next to the waterfalls and finally makes a steep climb up through the woods to reach the unpaved road just below the turnoff to Wiesenhof, approx. 1½ hrs. – To Wiesenhof (1058 m), turn left at Gasthof Brücke, go past the charming farms in Kumbichl to reach a farm road that climbs easily to the right, or go past this turnoff to the 'Alpenrose,' soon after which a forest trail cuts off to the right, approx. 1½ hrs. – To Penkenhaus (1814 m) with Penken Lift to mountain station and return over Gasthof (inn) Astegg, 3½ hrs. – Up to Rastkogel (2762 m) with Penken Lift to mountain station, across Wanglalm and over Wanglspitz (2420 m) to the peak. Return the same way, 6 hrs. – Up to Ahornspitze (2973 m) with Ahornbahn (lift) to Hahnpfalz and via Edelhütte (hut, 2238 m) to the peak, 3½ hrs. – Up to Kasseler Hütte (hut, 2718 m) from Gasthof Wasserfall (inn) on trail No. 515 to Grüne-Wand-Hütte (hut, 1436 m) and Kasseler Hütte, 2½ hrs.

RAMSAU im Zillertal E 1/F 13

Township, Schwaz County, Population: 1580, Elevation: 604 m, Postal Code: 6284. **Information:** Hippach – Ramsau – Schwendau Tourism Association. **Railroad Station:** Ramsau-Hippach. **Bus service:** from Jenbach, Mayrhofen, Zell am Ziller, Gerlos – Wald im Pinzgau. **Cable Lifts:** Chairlifts and towlifts.

The settlements making up Ramsau Township sprawl along the slopes of the Ramsberg, that is still densely wooded despite considerable clearing, or at its base on the east side of the upper Ziller Valley. Ramsau and Hippach share many tourism facilities. The Ramsberg Chairlift and numerous easy trails serve a hiking and relaxation park at a good elevation and with a beautiful view.

Attractions in Town and Nearby
The late neo-Classical **Church of the Seven Sorrows**, whose main altar is adorned with statues of Sts. Isidore and Notburga from 1770. – The **Old Mill Studio** (Studio Alte Mühle) of Max („Root Max") Hochmuth in Oberbichl, who earns his large family's livelihood as a painter, woodcarver, musician, mineral collector and dealer and, not least of all, as a Ziller Valley original.

Walks and Hikes
To Zell am Ziller on the Ziller-Promenade, 50 min., or along the foot of Ramsberg, through Schweiber and finally along the road, 1 hr. – To Mayrhofen on the Ziller-Promenade or through Unterbichl, Eckartau and Hollenzen, part of the way through a linden forest, 1 hr. – To Mayrhofen via top station of chairlift (Ramsberglift), Kotahornalm and Berggasthaus

Ziller Valley Railroad/Zillertalbahn/Il trenino della Zillertal

Steinerkogl (1270 m), 4½ – 5 hrs. – To the chairlift's middle station, from Ramsau by way of Jausenstation Waldheim, 1 hr. – To Gerlosstein-Berghotel (1620 m) via top station of chairlift (Ramsberglift), 2 hrs.

ROHRBERG   G 11

Township, Schwaz County, Population: 520, Elevation: approx 1000 m, Postal Code: 6280. **Information:** Zell – Gerlos Tourism Association. **Railroad Station:** Zell am Ziller, (from Rohr 1½ km). For further information, see Zell am Ziller.

The small town of mountain farmers primarily consists of scattered hamlets founded in the course of medieval forest clearing.

SCHWENDAU   E 1/F 13

Township, Schwaz County, Population: 1550, Elevation: 620 m, Postal Code: 6283. **Information:** Hippach – Ramsau – Schwendau Tourism Association. **Railroad Station:** Ramsau-Hippach (approx. 0.2 km). For **bus service** see Hippach. **Cabel Lift:** see Mayrhofen.

Schwendau is located on the side of the sunny valley, where it widens and the Sidanbach (brook) enters the main valley. The Sidanbach and Hoarbergbach (brooks) have carved deep beds in the soft quartz phyllite and washed up a broad alluvial fan that forced the Ziller River eastward. The town's name was first officially mentioned as „Swentouwe" around the year 1200 in the land register of Salzburg Archbishopric. This and other town names, such as Schwendberg and Stockach, document the extensive forest clearing undertaken by the early settlers. Schwendau was the home of the healer named Kiendler, whose reputation for herbal medicine reached far beyond the valley, even to Japan. He died in 1934, but tales are still told of some of his ingenious remedies, many of which are used and handed down today.

Attractions in Town and Nearby
The **Chapel of the Crucifixion** at Burgstallschrofen, erected in 1844. – **Keiler Waterfall.**

Walks
To Hippach ½ hr. – To Mayrhofen on the Ziller-Promenade via Mühlbach, Burgstall and Burgstallschrofen, ¾ hr. – To Keiler Waterfall 1 hr. – To Gasthof Zimmereben (restaurant), from Burgstall, 50 min.; descent to Mayrhofen or Finkenberg. – To Burgstall along Schwendauer Waldweg via Mühlen and back along the road, approx. 1½ hrs.

TUX   BC 2-4

Township, Schwaz County, Population: 1920, Elevation 1300 – 3476 m, Postal Code: 6293. **Information:** Tourist Office Tux – Finkenberg. **Railroad Station:** Mayrhofen (14 km). **Bus service:** to and from Mayrhofen and the bottom station of the Hintertuxer Gletscherbahnen in Hintertux. **Cable Lifts:** Hintertuxer Gletscherbahnen (hiking, summer and winter skiing with cable cars, chairlifts and towlifts), Eggalmbahn (quad lift).

Deep in the Ziller Valley at Mayrhofen (633 m) the Tux Valley branches off on its own. A winding but well built highway first leads to Finkenberg (839 m) and then crosses the Tuxbachklamm (gorge) on the mighty Rosengarten Bridge. From there it's only another 4 km to the Tux town line and the beginning of the beautiful Tux Valley. A drive into the Tux Valley takes you along good, safe, modern roads. The town of Tux spans an elevation of 1257 m (Vorderlanersbach) to 1493 m (Hintertux). The highest peak is the Olperer (3476 m). The five villages that make up the town of Tux, namely Hintertux, Madseit, Juns, Lanersbach and Vorderlanersbach, stretch out over 8 km. Guests as well as the local inhabitants love the idyllic Tux Valley all year round.

Until the mid 15th century, Hintertux belonged to Matrei in the Wipp Valley. It was only in 1926 that Hintertux split off from Schmirn. Since then Lanersbach, Lämperbichl and Hintertux have counted to today's town of Tux.

Sommerbergalm

Tux is also geologically important, because it forms the transition between the Tux Alps (shale bedrock) and the Tuxer Hauptkamm (granite-like gneis formations). At the back of the valley, at Hintertux, are the mighty Hintertux Glacier and the Olperer (3476 m), the valley's highest peak. The geological diversity on each side of the valley is what gives Tux its very special appearance and makes it popular with hikers and alpinists alike. Tux is situated in an unexposed location, which means the climate is much more mild than could be presume from the town's elevation and proximity to the glacier. The valley walls are green right up to the glacier, giving the valley the name „Green Glacier Valley." Long-term records kept by the meteorological service in Innsbruck show that each year Tux has on average: 1,839 hours of sun, 12 days with fog and 153 days with snow on the valley floor.

Sights Worth Seeing in Town and the Vicinity

From June to September grain is milled every Monday from 1 – 4 pm at the **Tuxer Mühle** in **Juns.** – The **Farming Museum** is located in the **Höllensteinhütte** and gives a good idea of the hard life of the mountain farmers and forest workers in Tux. – In **Madseit** the **Mehlerhof Farmstead** is a lovingly restored historic landmark. – Take the **valley hiking trail to „Drei Kreuze" in Hintertux**. – Near **Spannagelhaus**, 2531 m (10 minutes from the top station/Section II of the Hintertuxer Gletscherbahnen) is the natural monument **Spannagel Cave** (Spannagelhöhle). The cave is 4.2 km long and up to 25 m deep. It is Tyrol's largest cave and above all gives a good impression of the high-Alpine karstification of the glacier regions. A tour of the cave takes one hour. Guided tours available in summer and winter. – In **Gemais** above Vorderlanersbach are **farmsteads** from the 18th century which have been declared historic monuments. – At the **former magnesite works** on Schrofenalm is the **Chapel of St. Barbara** with the beautiful fresco painted by Max Weiler. – **Bergkäserei Stoankasern**, where cheese is made. – **Parish churches and chapels in the villages.** – **Tuxer Cascates.**

Hikes

There are 250 km of marked trails to alpine flowers, lakes, peaks and huts offering snacks. High-alpine tours, theme trails and guided hikes for 3 – 7 hrs. **Tip**: Wasserfallweg (circular tour to waterfall, approx. 1½ hrs.); moor nature trail, 2 hrs.; Theme trail with 9 signs (climate, water, geology, Alpine forests, avalanches, larch and spruce trees, Alpine pastures, glaciers and dry stone masonry); this 1-km-long trail connects the heart of Hintertux with the parking area of the Hintertux Glacier Cable Lift.

Hiking service: cable cars and hiking taxi as uphill short-cuts for dream panoramas, free hiking bus. Adventure glacier with hikes and climbing. Alpine sport school and mountain guides, adventure club with canyoning, cave trekking and Flying Fox, Kraxel-Maxel-Camp, ... Easy-going hikes from walks to challenging high-alpine tours; 17 alpine huts and snack restaurants (open from June to October).

Recommended Hikes

Bergstation Eggalm (1948 m) – Grüblspitze (2395 m) – Torsee (lake) – Lanersbach, 5 hrs. – Bergstation Eggalm (1948 m) – Waldhoar – Brandalm – Lanersbach, 2½ hrs. – Sommerbergalm – Frauenwand – Tuxer-Joch-Haus (2310 m) – Weitental – Hintertux, 4 hrs. – Hintertux – Spannagelhaus (2531 m) and Spannagelhöhle (cave), return by gondola lift, 3 hrs. walking time. – Lämmerbichl – Rastkogel (2762 m) – Vorderlanersbach, 6 hrs. – Bergkäserei Stoankasern – Junsjoch (2484 m) – Juns, 5 hrs.

ZELL am Ziller F 11

Market Town, Schwaz County, Population: 1770, Elevation: 575 m, Postal Code: 6280. **Information:** Zell – Gerlos Tourism Association. **Railroad Station:** Zell am Ziller. **Bus service:** from Jenbach and Mayrhofen, Gerlos – Wald im Pinzgau. **Cable Lifts:** Gondola lifts, chairlifts and towlifts.

Thanks to its good central location just south of the narrows separating the upper and the lower Ziller Valley, Zell on the Ziller has come to be the valley's thriving main town. The valley floor on both sides of the Ziller is well populated. As the name (Zelle or Cella) still shows, this was very early the site of a small monastery and church, whose property was conveyed to the settlement that is recorded in Salzburg Archbishopric's oldest land register (c. 1200) as one of the leading farms in the Zillertal. Zell later became the seat of the provost's court and since the 12th century it has been listed as one of Salzburg's two original parishes in the Ziller Valley. Zell's major role in valley affairs is anchored in the fact that, today too, the judicial, church and administrative authorities are located here as well as many local businesses. Every year in early May, Zell is the scene of the 'Gauderfest,' Tyrol's oldest spring festival, with music and dancing, wrestling and ram butting, with Gauder sausages and Gauder beer specially brewed in the town's own brewery, founded in 1500. The 'Gauderfest' was initiated about 400 years ago by the brewery's owners. There are plenty of other opportunities to experience the fun-loving nature of the Ziller Valley's populace, for ex. at carnival, when the cows are driven home from the summer pasture or at the famous Zeller Kirchtag (15.8.)

Attractions in Town and Nearby

Of the **Parish Church of St. Vitus** that probably originated in the 14th century, only the Gothic west tower remains; at the end of the 18th century A. Hueber added to it a lovely Rococo church designed on a central groundplan by W. Hagenauer; fresco fragment at the west side of the narthex; ceiling painting c. 1500; painting of St. Vitus by Franz Anton Zeiller at the main altar and presumably also the paintings (1779) at the side altars, baptismal font with Late Baroque carving in the narthex; cemetery with grave showing coat of arms of Johann Schoner and wife, deceased 1451. – **Maria Rast Pilgrimage Church, cheese-making demonstration, zoo** and **demonstration gold mine**: see Hainzenberg.

Walks and Hikes

See also adjoining sheet No. 28 „Vorderes Zillertal – Alpbach – Rofan – Wildschönau".
Circular walk from village square along Kraus-Promenade, from Rohrerstrasse to Gerlosstrasse, total approx. 1 hr. – To Mayrhofen on Ziller-Promenade along the east bank of the Ziller, 2 hrs.; return by way of Schwendau, Hippach and Laimach. – To Maria Rast along the way number 7, approx. 1½ hrs. – To Gerlosstein-Berghotel (1620 m) from Ötschenwirt (bus stop) or from the last large hairpin turn before Hainzenberg straight through the woods, approx. 2 – 2½ hrs.; many hikes possible from here, such as to Gerlossteinwand (2166 m), 1½ – 2 hrs.; to Arbiskögerl (1830 m), 1 hr.; to Mayrhofen via Kotahorn- and Labergalm – Berggasthaus Steinerkogl, approx. 3 hrs.

Township, Schwaz County, Population: 650, Elevation: 580 – 1000 m, Postal Code: 6280. **Information:** Zell – Gerlos Tourism Association. For further information, see Zell am Ziller.

The scattered communities on Zellberg were the seat of Salzburg's provost court at Zell. In religious matters, however, it belonged to Hippach Parish, because the Ziller River formed the border between the dioceses and the parishes.

High above the Ziller Valley/Hoch über dem Zillertal/Alti sulla valle Zillertal

One means of orientation is the **GPS** (Global Positioning System). A GPS device can determine your position (given in coordinates) anywhere in the world. This is done with the help of satellites circling the earth at an altitude of about 20,200 km and a speed of approx. 11,200 km/h that constantly give off signals. To use a GPS you should know the mapdatum and the ellipsoid of the particular country in order to receive the right coordinates. Working with a GPS device demands very good map reading skills and, above all, experience.

La carta escursionistica KOMPASS 1:25 000, foglio n. 037 „Mayrhofen - Tuxer Tal - Ziller-grund", riporta quel territorio alpino il cui centro è la nota stazione turistica di Mayrhofen. Qui si congiungono tutte le valli laterali della Zillertal per formare la larga valle principale che prosegue quasi diritta con andamento sud-nord e accoglie ancora presso Zell am Ziller (margine settentrionale della carta) la Gerlostal, ricca d'acqua, proveniente da est. Queste grandi vallate sorgive permettono l'accesso al grandioso mondo alpino che chiude in un largo cerchio l'alta Zillertal. I territori rivolti a sud verso la cresta principale delle Alpi si prestano ottimamente per escursioni ai grandi rifugi dell'Alpenverein, l'Associazione alpina austriaca, situati per lo più in fondo alla valle. Ad est di Mayrhofen si accede allo Zillergrund (collegamento taxibus) che a sua volta si articola in Zillergründl, Hundskehlgrund e Sundergrund. A sud si raggiunge lo Stillupgrund (strada a pedaggio fino al lago artificiale) superando un gradino vallivo. Presso Ginzling il Floitengrund permette l'accesso al cuore delle Alpi Zillertaler. Gunggl, Zemmgrund e lo Schlegeisgrund si susseguono in linea prima che lo Zamser Grund conduca al passo di Vizze, 2248 m, e quindi al confine con l'Alto Adige (Italia). Tra le valli Zamser e Tuxer si erge la cresta principale delle Alpi Tuxer con la cima Olperer, 3476 m, una delle più caratteristiche ad est del Brennero, riconoscibile già da lontano. A partire da Finkenberg la Tuxer Tal apre l'accesso alle Alpi Tuxer e alla zona sciistica aperta tutto l'anno del ghiacciaio Tuxer Ferner. Per il passo Gerlos, 1531 m, si hanno due possibilità di raggiungere Wald im Pinzgau, nella Salzachtal superiore: o si prende la strada panoramica a pedaggio con stupendi scorci sulle famose cascate di Krimml, oppure la strada di libero accesso che attraversa il pittoresco paesino di Königs-leiten.

Geologia

La bellezza delle Alpi Zillertaler con le creste principali delle Alpi Tuxer e Zillertaler ed il gruppo della Reichenspitze è data dalle audaci forme delle scure creste e cime in contrasto con il bianco luccicante dei ghiacciai, i cosiddetti „Keese", dai quali impetuosi torrenti si gettano nelle valli profondamente incise. Un paesaggio del tutto diverso lo incontriamo invece nelle Alpi Tuxer, prive di ghiacciai, che si collegano a nord. Questo contrasto è dovuto alla formazione geologica della montagna che evidenzia i seguenti raggruppamenti generalmente disposti da ovest ad est. Il nucleo delle Alpi Zillertaler è formato principalmente da gneis duri. Questa zona centrale di gneis inizia ad ovest con le ramificazioni della catena principale delle Alpi Tuxer e Zillertaler, che nella Stillupe si fondono in un'unica massa che continua in direzione est fino agli Alti Tauri. Il confine meridionale di questa zona percorre la Valle Aurina altoatesina e continua verso ovest fino al passo Ponte di Ghiaccio. A nord invece è delimitata dalla linea lungo il Kraxentrager – Kaserer – Mayrhofen – Krimml. Il nucleo di gneis è racchiuso ai due lati da un involucro di scisto, che ad ovest si infiltra anche tra le ramificazioni del gneis. La linea di confine settentrionale, raffigurata sul margine settentrionale della presente cartografia, si snoda da Matrei nella Wipptal attraverso Hippach fino al passo Gerlos. L'involucro è composto da rocce svariate, in prevalenza da scisti cristallini e viene suddiviso in due zone: una inferiore, più vicina al gneis centrale composta prevalentemente da rocce povere o prive di calcare, ed una superiore, esterna, nella quale sono fortemente presenti rocce ricche di calcare. All'escursionista farà piacere trovare una tale ricchezza di minerali, tra i quali meritano di essere menzionati i granati che venivano raccolti sul Rossrugg e poi frantumati in un „molino di granati" sul torrente poco sotto il rifugio Berliner Hütte. Nella zona di gneis, duro e resistente, l'erosione ha creato aguzze vette e creste taglienti che anche durante il periodo della massima glaciazione emergevano dalle imponenti masse di ghiaccio che sommersero le valli e le cime delle Alpi Tuxer e le appianarono. I ghiacci in movimento scavarono profondamente le valli dando loro quella tipica forma alla quale gli studiosi di glaciologia nelle Alpi Zillertaler, uno dei territori di

Grüblspitze, 2395 m

studio più antichi nella zona alpina, diedero il nome di valle ad U/Trogtal. Gli estesi circhi glaciali sul versante nord sono ancora oggi la fonte di alimentazione per enormi ghiacciai che a loro volta rivestono grande importanza per la produzione energetica quali serbatoi d'acqua. Sui versanti meridionali molto ripidi invece poterono formarsi solamente piccoli ghiacciai. Sui pendii e sui fondovalli si depositarono grandi quantità di materiale di disgregazione che veniva trasportato dai torrenti ricchi di acqua. Da sempre la Zillertal dovette subire le conseguenze catastrofiche di frane ed inondazioni. Ora si spera che questi problemi siano finalmente risolti grazie alla realizzazione di tre grandi invasi artificiali (Schlegeisspeicher, Speicher Stillup e Speicher Zillergründl), e con il risanamento dell'alveo del fiume nella valle principale.

Storia degli insediamenti

Il territorio raffigurato fino al confine con l'Italia appartiene politicamente al distretto di Schwaz della regione del Tirolo Settentrionale. Solo ad ovest fa capolino il comune di Schmirn del distretto di Innsbruck-Land, dal 1926 comunque solo fino al Tuxer Joch. A sudovest il comune di S. Giacomo di Vizze, nel comprensorio di Vipiteno, dopo la I guerra mondiale perdette il territorio a nord del passo di Vizze. La valle Aurina viene considerata appartenente alla val Pusteria con Brunico come centro principale. Il giogo del Cornetto/Hörndljoch, il passo del Cane/Hundskehljoch, e la forcella di Campo/Heilig-Geist-Jöchl, da sempre hanno consentito stretti legami con la Zillertal austriaca e le sue vallate laterali e ciò è dimostrato anche dal fatto che ancora oggi le malghe ed i pascoli sul versante austriaco appartengono ai contadini della valle Aurina, già in tempi remoti politicamente e fiscalmente legati alla Zillertal. Anche il rinvenimento dell'unico reperto preistorico fatto in questa zona, una spilla in bronzo, sul Tuxer Joch sembra confermare questa tesi, ma possiede comunque scarsa forza probatoria. La parte orientale della carta, con Krimml, fa parte del distretto Zell am See della regione di Salisburgo.

L'analisi sui toponimi ha portato alla conclusione che anche la Zillertal venne abitata da Illiri, più tardi romanizzati. Questa popolazione non molto numerosa fu poi completamente

51

integrata dai coloni Baiuvari spintisi fin qui nel VI sec. Molteplici toponimi di luoghi e località richiamano il lavoro di dissodamento e di bonifica testimoniando che i Bavari hanno assolto il più grande lavoro di colonizzazione. La valle venne menzionata in un atto ufficiale dell'889 allorché re Arnulf, contemporaneamente anche duca di Baviera, consegnò a Pilgrim, più tardi arcivescovo di Salisburgo, importanti possedimenti terreni nella „Cilarestal". Dominio feudale e potere comitale comunque qui non si integravano. Il torrente Ziller costituiva il confine tra le province romane della Rezia e del Norico e successivamente segnò a lungo il confine tra due contee. Quella ad ovest del torrente sottostò fin dall'XI sec. ai vescovi di Bressanone, passò poi ai conti di Andechs e dopo la loro estinzione andò agli Hirschberger e nel 1263 risp. 1282 ai conti di Tirolo. La parte orientale di questa contea fu data in feudo dagli Andechs ai loro seguaci, i signori di Rottenburg, la cui casa avita si trovava vicino a Jenbach. Da questo si sviluppò il tribunale Rottenburg che esercitò la piena giurisdizione fino ai confini orientali, presso lo Ziller. Ad est del torrente Ziller l'altra contea arrivava fino a Kufstein ed Erl, e venne retta dai conti bavaresi dai Rapotonen, dai vescovi di Regensburg e dal 1205 dai Wittelsbacher. Dalla loro „contea nelle montagne" si svilupparono i tribunali di Kufstein, di Kitzbühel e Rattenberg. Quest'ultimo esercitò l'alta giurisdizione fino allo Ziller. Dal 1290 al 1380 fu sotto il controllo dei reggenti tirolesi che lo poterono acquisire definitivamente assieme a Kitzbühel e Kufstein tramite l'imperatore Massimiliano I nel 1504. Furono però gli arcivescovi di Salisburgo a completare i loro possedimenti fino a comprendere quasi tutta la Zillertal. Già nel XII sec. vi crearono un apposito ufficio per amministrare i loro possedimenti nella Zillertal e dal 1200 circa esercitarono loro stessi i diritti di balivi. Alla fine del XIII sec. fecero erigere all'entrata della valle il castel Kropfsberg, a protezione della stessa, il cui curatore da allora in poi fu sempre il primo funzionario dell'arcivescovo della Zillertal.

Dato lo stretto legame tra proprietà e diritti nel corso dei secoli si ebbero varie controversie tra Salisburgo e Tirolo. I reggenti tirolesi, infatti, in base ai loro antichi diritti di contea, pretesero non solo la giurisdizione sulla vita e la morte nelle circoscrizioni giudiziarie della loro contea ma anche quelli economicamente importanti come il diritto sulle foreste, sulla caccia e sullo sfruttamento delle miniere. In effetti furono invece gli arcivescovi di Salisburgo ad esercitare nei loro territori su ambedue i lati dello Ziller quasi tutta la giurisdizione suprema, ad eccezione del diritto sulla vita e la morte, anche se spesso i funzionari di Salisburgo ignorarono volutamente la competenza dei tribunali di Rottenburg e Rattenberg. I Tirolesi riuscirono a far valere almeno in parte i loro diritti di regalia. Allorché nel 1803 tutti i principati ecclesiastici della Germania vennero secolarizzati, l'arcivescovado di Salisburgo passò al casato degli Asburgo e cioè prima alla linea collaterale della Toscana e solo nel 1805 direttamente all'impero austriaco. Contemporaneamente però con la cessione del Tirolo la Zillertal tirolese divenne bavarese e fu così che le antiche controversie continuarono ora con le parti invertite. Gli ex comuni salisburghesi parteciparono convintamente alla guerra di liberazione tirolese del 1809. Andreas Hofer concluse con essi un trattato con il quale tutta la Zillertal doveva essere unita al Tirolo. Questa unione avvenne poi comunque sotto la reggenza bavarese in quanto l'Austria dopo la sua sconfitta dovette cedere alla Baviera anche il Salisburghese. Questa regolamentazione durò ben poco, poiché la Baviera dopo il Congresso di Vienna dovette restituire le intere acquisizioni all'Austria. Nel 1816 su ordine dell'imperatore Francesco I la Zillertal salisburghese e la Brixental venivano definitivamente unite al Tirolo. Questa unione era ben voluta dalla popolazione che da sempre si sentiva appartenente al Tirolo. Dal punto di vista ecclesiastico rimase invece la divisione tuttora in atto. Lo Ziller è rimasto la linea di confine tra i due vescovadi: le parrocchie salisburghesi sulla destra del torrente con i campanili verdi (decanato di Zell am Ziller), quelle della diocesi di Innsbruck sulla sinistra con i campanili rossi (decanato di Fügen).

Circostanze sfavorevoli portarono presto allo spopolamento della valle la cui base agricola non riuscì a far fronte alle esigenze dell'aumento demografico della popolazione. Commer-

Scorci idilliaci/Herrliche Ausblicke beim Wandern/Hikes with unbeatable views

cianti della Zillertal divennero venditori ambulanti attraverso tutto il paese. Inizialmente già nel XVI sec. vendevano prodotti agricoli eccedenti come lardo, formaggi e bestiame nei comuni limitrofi, poi pian piano il commercio si allargò anche ad altre merci. Godeva di buona fama la grappa della Zillertal per la cui produzione e vendita erano necessari ricercatori di radici, distillatori e venditori. Particolarmente noti erano anche i commercianti di guanti della Zillertal le cui merci non venivano quasi mai prodotte nella valle. Nel XVII e XVIII sec. i cosiddetti portatori d'olio sostenevano un proficuo commercio con varie creme, olii e tinture per l'uomo e le bestie, ma spesso il compratore veniva letteralmente imbrogliato da ciarlatani.

La rigidezza nelle questioni di coscienza e religione indusse nel 1837 ben 400 uomini prevalentemente dei comuni della valle superiore del Finkenberg e Brandberg a lasciare la patria, in quanto la Dieta tirolese, in ted. Tiroler Landtag, non riconobbe la „patente di tolleranza" dell'imperatore Giuseppe II. Gli emigranti poterono stabilirsi in gruppo nella Slesia prussiana costruendo il villaggio Zillertal, che per loro costituiva un pezzo di patria, fino a quando nel 1945 vennero nuovamente scacciati. La fermezza del contegno di questi emigranti suscitò ammirazione in tutta Europa e contribuì a rendere nota questa valle oltreconfine. Fin dal 1820 gruppi musicali e famiglie di cantori come i Rainer, i Leo, gli Strasser e gli Hollaus pubblicizzarono in tutta Europa la loro bella valle che già allora stava iniziando a suscitare l'interesse dei primi turisti. L'attività turistica aumentò sensibilmente dal 1850 con la scoperta dell'alpinismo e delle montagne e costituisce oggi con l'agricoltura l'introito principale dell'economia locale. Manca invece l'industria e solo nelle grandi località vallive in tempi più recenti si sono sviluppate strutture industriali, che però non pregiudicano il paesaggio. Un sostanziale intervento sul paesaggio è stato invece causato dalla realizzazione della centrale elettrica, che ha lesionato l'autenticità dei terreni interessati. Nuove attrazioni sono i bacini artificiali di Schlegeis, Stillup e Zillergründl.

L'industria mineraria un tempo molto diffusa è ormai completamente inesistente. La miniera d'oro sull'Hainzenberg, ora aperta al pubblico, rimase in funzione fino alla seconda metà del XIX sec. La presenza di granati sul Rossrugg venne scoperta a metà del XVIII sec. da un contadino cacciatore di frodo. In seguito le belle pietre vennero raccolte regolarmente per quasi cent'anni, poi pulite in un apposito mulino nello Zemmgrund e quindi vendute a ditte boeme che le intagliavano e levigavano. Nel 1836 l'impianto venne chiuso. Solo la miniera di rame presso Predoi in Valle Aurina fu riattivata dal 1959 al 1971 in scarsa misura. Ora ospita una delle sedi del Museo Provinciale delle Miniere dell'Alto Adige. Furono invece attivati dopo la prima guerra mondiale i giacimenti di magnesio e scheelite al di sopra di Lanersbach che diedero lavoro ad alcune centinaia di persone fino alla chiusura nel 1976. Il costume tipico del luogo – corpetto in velluto nero con scialle in seta chiara e stesso grembiule sopra una gonna nera per donne e ragazze, calzoni alla zuava in pelle nera e giacchetta in loden grigio con guarnizioni in nero sopra la camicia bianca e grembiulone rosso per gli uomini, e per ambedue i sessi un bel cappello nero con nappa dorata – viene portato ancora volentieri in occasione di festività religiose e non.

Fauna e Flora

Gli abitanti della Zillertal sono cacciatori appassionati. Infatti furono completamente sterminati gli stambecchi. Gli ultimi stambecchi furono traslocati per opera dell'arcivescovo di

Salisburgo agli inizi del XVIII sec. Buona è invece ancora la consistenza di camosci. I cervi sono numerosi soprattutto nella zona di Gerlos dove possono essere osservati poco lontano dal paese in occasione del foraggiamento. I fischi delle marmotte sono udibili nelle zone solitarie ma è raro adocchiarne una. I caprioli sono presenti dal fondovalle fino al limite boschivo e pure il gallo ce-

Rododendro in fiore/Alpenrosenblüte/Alpine roses in blossom

drone ed il fagiano di monte sono presenti in tutta la valle. Per la gioia dei pescatori i limpidi torrenti sono ricchi di trote. Nonostante il forte disboscamento la valle è ancora ricca di bellissimi boschi. L'albero più frequente è l'abete, mentre merita una menzione il cirmolo che dimora presso il limite superiore del bosco. La flora è molto varia e consta di quasi tutte le specie di fiori alpini la cui ubicazione dipende dalle condizioni climatiche e del terreno. Come in tutto il resto del Tirolo le specie più rare sono protette. Particolarmente protetto è il bosco Scheulingwald presso Mayrhofen nonché il boschetto di tigli, in ted. Lindenwäldchen, presso Ramsau, ed il boschetto misto di tigli e faggi, soprannominato in tedesco „Glocke" (con percorso didattico naturalistico) a Finkenberg.

Sentieri a lunga percorrenza

La sezione dell'Associazione alpina che cura i sentieri a lunga percorrenza è il centro informazioni a cui rivolgersi per quanto concerne i sentieri europei ed i sentieri a lunga percorrenza in territorio austriaco.
Informazioni: Österreichischer Alpenverein, Sektion Weitwanderer, Thaliastraße 159/3/16, 1160 Vienna, Austria, tel. e fax 0043/(0)1/4938408, cellulare 0664/2737242,
weitwanderer@sektion.alpenverein.at
www.alpenverein.at/weitwanderer • www.fernwege.de
Le associazioni alpine hanno provveduto ad apportare la segnaletica, contraddistinta da un numero e da un nome, lungo i sentieri a lunga percorrenza allo scopo di informare gli escur-

sionisti su mete locali di interesse, fino ad allora poco ricercate, ma meritevoli.

Per facilitare l'utilizzazione di detti percorsi è stata edita una guida che informa il lettore sul percorso, le possibilità di pernottamento, la distanza in chilometri ed il dislivello, il tempo di percorrenza ed il grado di difficoltà così come anche sugli orari di apertura degli alberghi e dei rifugi. Sono stati inoltre istituiti posti di controllo, dove poter timbrare la visita e far quindi richiesta degli appositi distintivi escursionistici per il tratto percorso, indipendentemente dal tempo impiegato.

Oltre ai numerosi itinerari regionali l'Austria offre anche ben **10 sentieri a lunga percorrenza**, contrassegnati da 01 a 10. L'eventuale presenza di un numero al posto del centinaio indica il gruppo montuoso. Nelle Alpi Centrali il numero è dispari (ad es. 901), mentre nelle Alpi Calcaree settentrionali e meridionali esso è pari (ad es. 801). La presenza di una lettera dopo il numero indica invece la variante del sentiero. Numerosi sentieri nazionali a lunga percorrenza sono integrati nella rete dei sentieri europei.

La presente carta riporta il sentiero delle Alpi Centrali n. 02.

Prima di intraprendere un'escursione si consiglia di informarsi sulle possibilità o meno di pernottamento nei rifugi o nelle località indicate. I sentieri a lunga percorrenza richiedono esperienza di montagna, buone condizioni fisiche ed un buon equipaggiamento.

Sviluppo dei sentieri a lunga percorrenza
Il Sentiero delle Alpi centrali n. 02/Sentiero principale n. 502:

Il Sentiero delle Alpi centrali n. 02 ha inizio a Hainburg an der Donau, giunge fino a Feldkirch in Vorarlberg attraversando tutte le regioni austriache eccetto l'Austria superiore e Vienna. È il più alpino di tutti i sentieri a lunga percorrenza e si snoda per ca. 1000 km. Dato che questo percorso si svolge in alta montagna – a tratti anche attraverso ghiacciai! – sono assolutamente necessari esperienza d'alta montagna, buone condizioni fisiche ed un adeguato equipaggiamento! Esperte guide alpine nelle località a valle potranno offrirvi sicurezza durante il tragitto. Chiedete informazioni all'associazione turistica. Vi raccomandiamo di informarVi sullo stato attuale dei sentieri che volete percorrere e sulla possibilità o meno di pernottamento nei rifugi che toccherete prima di metterVi in cammino .

Il sentiero entra sul margine destro della carta (quadrante di riferimento K 17), proveniente dal rif. Warnsdorfer Hütte, oltrepassa la forcella Zillerplattenscharte e giunge al rif. Plauener Hütte. Prosegue oltre il bacino artificiale Zillergründl seguendo la strada verso l'uscita della valle, toccando gli alberghi Bärenbad, In der Au, Häusling e Klaushof prima di arrivare nei pressi di Mayrhofen. Lungo la strada ci si avvicina al bacino artificiale Stillup. Oltrepassato il rif. Stillupphaus si sale al rif. Grüne-Wand-Hütte, indi più ripidi al rif. Kasseler Hütte. Con un ampio arco il sentiero aggira alcuni tremila e un ghiacciaio dopo l'altro, sale alla forcella Lapenscharte e scende quindi al rif. Greizerhütte. Il percorso scende attraverso il Floitengrund e per scalette – necessari passo sicuro e mancanza di vertigini – sale ripido alla forcella Mörchenscharte, indi altrettanto irto al circo glaciale Rosskar ed al lago Nero, in ted. Schwarzensee, per giungere infine al rif. Berliner Hütte. Seguono passaggi impegnativi, assicurati con funi e molto esposti, lungo la cresta Schönbichler Grat e oltre, sul sentiero Berliner Höhenweg al rif. Furtschaglhaus. In serpentine si scende al bacino artificiale Schlegeisgrund e per la carrareccia lo si segue fino allo Zamser Grund. Da lì il sentiero delle Alpi centrali devia per un sentierino che lo conduce al rif. Olpererhütte. Irto ed impegnativo prosegue sulla cresta Riepengrat alla forcella Alpeiner Scharte e – in discesa con la massima prudenza – al rif. Geraer Hütte, dove esce dalla presente cartografia (A 7) per Vals.

Il Sentiero delle Alpi centrali n. 02 – Variante n. 702A, 502A, 302A

Per evitare passaggi molto difficili del percorso principale sono state create delle varianti. Anch'esse portano quasi esclusivamente in alta montagna – a tratti attraverso ghiacciai! – e sono quindi indispensabili esperienza d'alta montagna, buone condizioni fisiche ed un adeguato equipaggiamento! (V. introduzione al sentiero principale).

Il sentiero delle Alpi centrali della presente cartografia presenta la variante n. 702A, 502A e 302A dal paesino di malghe di Königsleiten, che dal margine superiore destro (quadrante di riferimento K 11) prosegue per Gerlos, Gmünd, Hainzenberg e Maria Rast fino a Hippach. Lungo la strada d'alta montagna (Zillertaler-Höhenstraße) fino a Grün, dove esce dalla carta per recarsi al rif. Rastkogelhütte (D 1), e rientrare poco dopo nel quadrante di riferimento C 1. Si può seguire il sentiero per un breve tratto sul margine superiore della carta, al Rastkogel, prima che si diriga al rif. Weidener Hütte (B 1) ed esca nuovamente dalla carta. Rientra un'ultima volta sulla carta nel quadrante di riferimento A 1, per salire al giogo Krovenzjoch ed al rif. Lizumer Hütte, nei pressi della zona per le esercitazioni militari di Lizum-Walchen, prosegue per il Geier e vicino al Lizumer Reckner, per poi uscire definitivamente dalla carta nel quadrante di riferimento A 3 in direzione di Navis.

Alte vie

Alpi Tuxer
Con condizioni sicure da slavine i passaggi sono consigliabili anche per lo sci-alpinismo.

1° giorno:
a) Punto di partenza stazione a monte della funivia Penken o Gschößwandhaus; da Mayrhofen a piedi, ore 3-3.30; attraverso il Gschößberg al rif. Penkenjochhaus, 2095 m, ore 1.15, più oltre alla Wanglalm e per la Wanglspitz, 2420 m, e l'Hoarbergjoch, 2590 m, per lastroni di pietre alla cima del Rastkogel, 2762 m, totale ore 3.30-4.
b) Punto di partenza rif. Rastkogelhütte, raggiungibile da Hippach, ore 4-4.30, risp. dall'albergo Mösl (fermata autobus), ore 1.30-2; dal rifugio per la Sidanalm alla forcella a sud-est del Rastkogel, 2762 m, e poi alla vetta, ore 2; dalla cima lungo la cresta ovest oppure un po' più a sud di questa al Nurpensjoch dal quale si raggiunge facilmente la Halslspitze, 2574 m, e poi per la Nafingalm al rif. Weidener Hütte (Nafinghütte, 1856 m), ore 2 ca.

2° giorno:
Si veda anche il foglio limitrofo n. 37 „Zillertaler Alpen - Tuxer Alpen".
a) Dal rif. Weidener Hütte attraverso il Geiseljoch, 2292 m, alla Geiselalm, ore 2.30; da lì poi per la Nasse Tuxalm al Torjoch, 2386 m, passando per i laghi Torseen, ore 2.30; discesa al rif. Lizumer Hütte, 2019 m, 30 min., totale ore 5.30-6.
b) Dal rif. Weidener Hütte attraverso la Grafennsalm al Grafennsjoch, 2450 m, a nord della Hippoldspitze, 2642 m, ore 3; si può raggiungere facilmente la vetta da ovest. Si scende per l'Außerlann-Hochleger ed il Niederleger alla Innerlannalm e da qui lungo il magnifico sentiero dei cirmoli, in ted. Zirbenweg, si sale al rif. Lizumer Hütte, 2019 m, ca. ore 2.30.

3° giorno:
Dal rif. Lizumer Hütte sempre in direzione sud, oltrepassando il laghetto Junssee, fino alla panoramica alta via per il rif. Tuxer-Joch-Haus, 2310 m, ore 5-6. Proseguimento dell'escursione verso ovest, vedi foglio limitrofo n. 36 „Innsbruck - Brenner" o discesa ad Hintertux, ore 2.

Alpi Zillertaler
Grande attraversata ovest-est (in gran parte su sentieri dell'Alpenverein)

1° giorno:
Salita al rif. Geraer Hütte, 2326 m; da St. Jodok am Brenner (vedi foglio limitrofo n. 36 „Innsbruck - Brenner") lungo la valle Valsertal all'albergo Touristenrast, ore 1.30-2; quindi si segue il torrente Alpeiner Bach (fine della strada praticabile) e con tornanti si supera il ripido gradino per arrivare al rif. Ochsnerhütte, 2081 m, poi più pianeggiante attraverso i pascoli della malga Alpeiner Alm fino al Windschaufelgraben, lungo questo in ripida salita e con tornanti al rifugio, totale ca. ore 4.30.

1° giorno - variante:

Salita al rif. Tuxer-Joch-Haus, 2310 m: a) da St. Jodok attraverso la Schmirntal a Kasern, ca. ore 2.30; più oltre al Kaserer Winkl, dove termina la strada praticabile, 30 min. ed in altre 2 ore su mulattiera al rifugio, totale ca. ore 4.30-5; b) meno faticoso da Hintertux, ore 2.30, approfittando della seggiovia Sommerbergalm, 45 min.

2° giorno:

Dal rifugio si sale lungo il margine sinistro del ghiacciaio Alpeiner Ferner (miniera in disuso) alla forcella Alpeiner Scharte, 2959 m, ore 2. Si continua però scendendo ripidamente nel circo glaciale dell'Unterschrammach con piccoli laghetti e nella conca Zamser Grund, attraverso la quale si cammina verso l'uscita della valle al bacino artificiale Schlegeisspeicher (possibilità di arrivare al rif. Dominikus, 1805 m, 15 min., fermata autobus), ore 2-2.30; quindi per l'alta via Berliner Höhenweg lungo la riva del lago per la conca Schlegeisgrund fino al Furtschaglboden e per tornanti al rif. Furtschaglhaus, 2295 m, ore 2.30, totale ore 7 ca.

2° giorno - variante:

Traversata al rif. Spannagelhaus, 2531 m, ore 2; poi attraverso la forcella Friesenbergscharte, 2910 m, facilmente al rif. Friesenberghaus, 2498 m, presso il lago Friesenbergsee, ca. ore 3.30; da qui si continua o direttamente al bacino artificiale Schlegeisspeicher, ore 1.30, oppure si fa un giro per il rif. Olpererhütte, 2388 m, ore 2, ed in un'altra buona ora si scende al lago artificiale. Qui si incontra il sentiero che conduce al rif. Furtschaglhaus, vedi sopra. Questa variante può essere abbreviata solo approfittando delle seggiovie da Hintertux.

3° giorno:

Dal rif. Furtschaglhaus al panoramico Schönbichler Horn, 3134 m, ore 2.30-3; dalla forcella in direzione est ripidamente (assicurazione con corde) lungo il fianco alla cresta e attraverso questa su un comodo sentiero lastricato si scende alla lingua del ghiacciaio Waxeggkees completamente prosciugata; il sentiero attraversa gli imponenti depositi morenici ai piedi dei ghiacciai Waxeggkees e Hornkees ed infine sale in breve al rif. Berliner Hütte, 2042 m, totale ore 5-6.

4° giorno:

Si passa per il lago Schwarzensee, in bellissima posizione, e si giunge nel Rosskar (a sinistra deviazione per la forcella Melkerscharte) e per serpentine si raggiunge la forcella Mörchenscharte settentrionale, 2957 m, ore 2.30-3; poi si scende con molte ripide serpentine (assicurazione con funi) fino al Floitengrund superiore che si attraversa incontrando sull'altro versante vallivo il sentiero che in circa 45 min. sale al rif. Greizerhütte, 2227 m, totale ore 5.30.

5° giorno:

Per i pendii del Griesfeld in direzione nord, poi in serpentine alla forcella Lapenscharte, 2701 m, ore 1.30; al di là si passa sotto le rocce del Gigalitz scendendo allo schienale morenico e al circo glaciale Lapenkar fino alla biforcazione; a destra una bella alta via (assicurazione con funi) conduce attraverso i circhi glaciali della Stillupgrund superiore al rif. Kasseler Hütte, 2178 m, totale ore 4.30-5; a sinistra si scende attraverso il Lapenkar e passando per il Lapenhütte (in disuso) e tra i torrenti, molto ripidamente, nello Stillupgrund; si attraversa un ponte per arrivare alla Taxachalm ed al rif. Grüne-Wand-Hütte, 1436 m, totale ore 4-4.30.

6° giorno:

Attraverso lo Stillupgrund al limite settentrionale del bacino artificiale, dal rif. Kasseler Hütte ca. ore 3.30-4; da qui si passa per la Krötzelbergalm e Hahnpfalz al rif. Edelhütte, 2238 m, ore 3-3.30.

7° giorno:
Attraverso la Ahornachalm e la Stadelbachalm si giunge all'albergo alpino Häusling, 1053 m, nella Zillergrund, ore 4; addentrandosi nella valle si raggiunge l'albergo In der Au, ore 1.30 (eventualmente possibilità di viaggio in macchina), più oltre all'albergo Bärenbad, 45 min. Servizio navetta (Shuttle-Bus) al ristorante Adlerblick. Camminatori allenati possono salire per il ristorante Adlerblick ed il bacino artificiale Zillergründl lungo il sentiero Dreiländer-Weg al rif. Plauener Hütte, 2364 m, ore 2.30; da lì è possibile continuare l'escursione per il rif. Richterhütte, 2367 m, e più oltre verso nord passando per il rif. Zittauer Hütte a Gerlos oppure verso est per il rif. Krimmler Tauernhaus, 1631 m, nel gruppo montuoso del Gran Veneziano, vedi foglio limitrofo n. 38 „Venedigergruppe - Oberpinzgau".

 Via Alpina Con 341 tappe giornaliere, 5 diversi itinerari e oltre 5000 km di sentieri la Via Alpina invita alla scoperta di otto stati alpini: Principato di Monaco, Francia, Svizzera, Liechtenstein, Germania, Austria, Italia e Slovenia. Il percorso si svolge da Monaco a Trieste ad un'altitudine che varia da 0 a 3000 m lungo tutto l'arco alpino, attraverso 9 parchi nazionali, 17 parchi naturali, innumerevoli zone sotto tutela ambientale ed oltrepassa ben 60 volte i confini dei vari stati. Non presenta difficoltà tecniche notevoli ed è quindi agibile durante l'estate senza corde o ramponi, ma adeguatamente equipaggiati. Ogni tappa offre varie possibilità di pernottamento a valle o nei rifugi dei club alpini.
La convenzione stipulata dagli Stati alpini nel 1991 ha realizzato questo progetto allo scopo di incrementare durevolmente lo sviluppo e la presa di coscienza necessaria per la tutela dell'area alpina, così ecologicamente sensibile. Le Alpi infatti non rappresentano soltanto l'area naturale più grande d'Europa che dà rifugio e protezione ad innumerevoli specie di flora e fauna endemica di rara bellezza, bensì offre spazio anche a 13 milioni di persone, a popolazioni caratterizzate da tradizioni plurisecolari e da scambi culturali.
Sul sito www.via-alpina.org troverete ulteriori informazioni.

Adlerweg - Escursionismo sulle ali dell'aquila

Il principale sentiero escursionistico del Tirolo, l'Adlerweg, o „sentiero dell'aquila", attraversa tutta la regione prevalentemente da est ad ovest: da St. Johann nel Tiroler Unterland oltrepassa il Wilder Kaiser, prosegue attraverso le Alpi Brandenberger, i massicci montuosi del Rofan e del Karwendel e le Alpi Lechtaler fino a St. Anton am Arlberg. Questo percorso assomiglia a grandi tratti alla silhouette di un'aquila. Le varianti locali conducono nelle valli laterali della Valle dell'Inn – Paznauntal, Kaunertal, Pitztal, Ötztal, Stubaital e Zillertal –, come anche a Tannheim, nel Kaiserwinkl e nelle Alpi di Kitzbühel. La „giovane aquila" nel Tirolo Orientale – come anche l'aquila del Tirolo settentrionale – offrono all'escursionista tutta la vasta gamma dell'escursionismo in montagna, dal percorso impegnativo in alta montagna alla piacevole passeggiata. Con una segnaletica uniforme, ben marcato e descritto dettagliatamente, il sentiero dell'aquila porta attraverso l'avvincente paesaggio tirolese ai posti più belli della regione. Provare per credere!
Ulteriori informazioni sul sito www.adlerweg.tirol.at in lingua tedesca ed in inglese.

Sosta al lago Torsee/Rast am Torsee/Taking a break at Torsee

Elenco degli Alberghi e Rifugi Alpini

Non ci assumiamo responsabilità alcuna per le indicazioni fornite. Prima di iniziare le escursioni informarsi a valle sul periodo di apertura dei rifugi e sulla possibilità o meno di pernottamento.
Troverete l'elenco dei numeri telefonici dei più importanti alberghi alpini e rifugi a pag. 76.

Alpi Tuxer

Astegg, 1176 m (D 2), albergo, privato, CAP: 6292 Finkenberg, aperto tutto l'anno. Accessi: da Finkenberg, ore 1; da Mayrhofen, ore 2. Traversate: al rif. Penkenhaus, ore 1.30; al rif. Gschößwandhaus, ore 2.

Bergrast, 1794 m (D 2), albergo sul Gschößberg, v. Gschößwandhaus.

Eggalm, 1948 m (B 3), ristorante, privato, CAP: 6293 Lanersbach, aperto tutto l'anno. Accesso: da Lanersbach, ore 2.15, oppure con l'ovovia. Traversata: al rif. Lizumer Hütte, ore 4. Cima: Grüblspitze, 2395 m, ore 1 (facile).

Gschößwandhaus (Rifugio), 1762 m (D 2), stazione a monte della funivia Penkenbahn, privato, CAP: 6290 Mayrhofen, aperto tutto l'anno. Accessi: da Finkenberg, circa ore 3; da Mayrhofen, ore 3-3.30. Traversate: al rif. Penkenjochhaus per il Gschößberg, ore 1.15; al rif. Penkenhaus, ore 1.15; all'albergo Mösl, ore 1.30. Cima: Gschößberg, 2005 m, 30 min. (facile).

Lizumer Hütte (Rifugio), 2019 m (A 2), Alpenverein, CAP: 6112 Wattens, aperto nella stagione invernale ed estiva. Accessi: da Wattens, ore 5; da Walchen (fin lì in auto), ore 2. Traversate: a Lanersbach, ore 3.30; al rif. Weidener Hütte per il giogo Krovenzjoch, ore 5; al rif. Tuxer-Joch-Haus, ore 6. Cime: Mölser Sonnenspitze, 2427 m, ore 2 (facile); Geier, 2857 m, ore 3 (facile); Lizumer Reckner, 2886 m, ore 3.30 (solo per esperti).

Penkenhaus (Rifugio), 1814 m (D 2), privato, CAP: 6292 Finkenberg, aperto tutto l'anno. Accessi: da Mayrhofen, ore 3.45; da Finkenberg, ore 2.30-3; dalla stazione a monte della funivia Penkenbahn, ore 1.15. Traversata: al rif. Penkenjochhaus, 45 min.

Penkenjochhaus (Rifugio), 2095 m (D 2), privato, CAP: 6292 Finkenberg, aperto tutto l'anno. Accessi: da Finkenberg per il rif. Penkenhaus, ore 3.30; da Mayrhofen, ore 4-4.30; dalla stazione a monte della funivia Penkenbahn, ore 1.15. Traversate: per la Schrofenalm a Vorderlanersbach, ore 2.30; al rif. Rastkogelhütte, per il Rastkogel, ore 4 ca. Cime: Wanglspitz, 2420 m, ore 1.30 (facile); Rastkogel, 2762 m, ore 3 (facile).

Perler (Albergo alpino), 1130 m (D 1), privato, CAP: 6283 Hippach, aperto tutto l'anno. Accesso: da Hippach, ore 1.30, accesso in macchina. Traversata: al rif. Rastkogelhütte, ore 3.

Alpi Zillertaler

(Tuxer Hauptkamm, Zillertaler Hauptkamm e Gruppo della Reichenspitze)

Adlerblick, 1900 m (I 16), ristorante, privato, CAP: 6290 Mayrhofen, aperto in estate. Accesso: con l'auto o l'autobus fino a Bärenbad; indi o a piedi in 45 min. o con il servizio navetta. Nei pressi la nuova cappella.

Alpenrose (Albergo), 1398 m (E 3, F 15), privato, CAP: 6290 Mayrhofen, aperto in estate. Accesso: da Mayrhofen, ore 2-2.30. Traversata: al rif. Edelhütte ore 2.30.

Alpenrosehütte (Rifugio), 1873 m (D 8), privato, CAP: 6295 Ginzling, aperto in estate. Accesso: da Ginzling, ore 4.30; dall'albergo Breitlahner, fermata autobus, ore 2.30. Traversate: al rif. Berliner Hütte, 30 min.; al rif. Furtschaglhaus, ore 5.30-6.

Bärenbad, 1450 m (I 16), privato, CAP: 6290 Mayrhofen, aperto in estate. Accesso: da Mayrhofen, ore 4.45; anche in auto (strada a pedaggio - traffico limitato) o con l'autobus. Traversata: al rif. Plauener Hütte, ore 2.

Berliner Hütte (Rifugio), 2042 m (D 8), Alpenverein, CAP: 6295 Ginzling, aperto in estate. Accesso: da Ginzling, ore 4.30-5, dall'albergo Breitlahner, fermata autobus, ore 3 ca. Traversate: al rif. Alpenrosehütte, 20 minuti; al rif. Greizerhütte per la forcella Nördliche Mörchenscharte, ore 5.30-6; al rif. Furtschaglhaus per il Schönbichler Horn, ore 6; nel Gunggl per la forcella Melkerscharte, ore 6-7. Cima: Schönbichler Horn, 3134 m, ore 4. Numerose escursioni d'alta quota di ogni grado di difficoltà.

Brandberger Kolmhaus (Rifugio), 1845 m (G 14), privato, CAP: 6290 Mayrhofen, aperto in estate. Accessi: da Brandberg, ore 2 ca.; da Mayrhofen, ore 3.30-4. Traversate: nella Gerlostal all'albergo Kühle Rast (fermata autobus) per il giogo Brandberger Joch, ore 3.30; all'albergo alpino Gerlosstein, ore 2.30. Cime: Brandberger Kolm, 2700 m, ore 2.30-3 (difficoltà media); Torhelm, 2452 m, ore 2 (facile).

Breitlahner (Albergo), 1256 m (C 6), privato, CAP: 6295 Ginzling, aperto in estate. Accesso: da Ginzling, ore 2; con la macchina o l'autobus fino all'albergo. Traversate: al rif. Berliner Hütte, ore 3; al rif. Dominikushütte, ore 2; al rif. Friesenberghaus, ore 4.

Dominikushütte (Rifugio), 1805 m (B 7), privato, CAP: 6295 Ginzling, aperto in estate. Accessi: in auto (strada a pedaggio!) o autobus fino al rifugio; da Ginzling, ore 4.30; dall'albergo Breitlahner, ore 2. Traversate: al rif. Passo di Vizze, ore 2; al rif. Friesenberghaus, ore 2.30; al rif. Olpererhütte, ore 2; al rif. Furtschaglhaus, ore 2.30. Cima: Olperer, 3476 m, ore 5 (solo per esperti).

Edelhütte (Rifugio), 2238 m (E 4, F 16), Alpenverein, CAP: 6290 Mayrhofen, aperto in estate. Accessi: da Mayrhofen, ore 4.30-5; dalla stazione a monte della funivia Ahornbahn, ore 1. Traversate: nella Stillupgrund al rif. Stilluphaus, ore 2.30. Cima: Ahornspitze, 2973 m, ore 2-2.30 (solo per esperti).

Finkau (Trattoria), 1420 m (K 13), privato, CAP: 5743 Krimml, aperto tutto l'anno. Accessi: in macchina fino alla casa oppure a piedi dal passo Gerlos, ore 2; da Gerlos, ore 3. Traversata: al rif. Zittauer Hütte, ore 3.

Friesenberghaus (Rifugio), 2498 m (B 6), Alpenverein, CAP: 6295 Ginzling, aperto in estate. Accessi: dall'albergo Breitlahner, ore 3.30; dal rif. Dominikushütte, ore 2. Traversate: al rif. Spannagelhaus attraverso la forcella Friesenbergscharte, ore 3; al rif. Olpererhütte, ore 2, solo su tracce di sentiero (solo per esperti); Petersköpfl, 2679 m, 45 min. (facile).

Furtschaglhaus (Rifugio), 2295 m (C 9), Alpenverein, CAP: 6295 Ginzling, aperto in estate. Accesso: dal rif. Dominikushütte, ore 2.30. Traversate: al rif. Berliner Hütte per il Schönbichler Horn, ore 6.30. Cima: Schönbichler Horn, 3134 m, ore 2.30 (difficoltà media). Numerose escursioni d'alta quota di ogni grado di difficoltà.

Gamshütte (Rifugio), 1921 m (D 4), Alpenverein, CAP: 6290 Mayrhofen, aperto in estate. Accessi: da Finkenberg, ore 3; da Ginzling, ore 3. Cime: Grinbergspitzen, 2884 m, 2765 m e 2867 m, circa ore 2.30 (difficoltà media).

Geraer Hütte (Rifugio), 2324 m (A 7), Alpenverein, CAP: 6154 St. Jodok am Brenner, aperto in estate. Accesso: da St. Jodok, ore 4.30; in macchina o autobus fino alla trattoria Touristenrast, da lì ore 2.30. Traversate: al rif. Olpererhütte, ore 4; per il sentiero Wildlahnerweg a Schmirn, ore 2.30; per la forcella Kleegrubenscharte al rif. Tuxer-Joch-Haus, ore 4-4.30.

Gerlosstein-Berghotel (Albergo alpino), 1620 m (G 13), privato, CAP: 6280 Hainzenberg, aperto tutto l'anno. Accessi: nelle vicinanze della stazione a monte della funivia Gerlossteinbahn; da Hainzenberg, fermata autobus Ötschenwirt, ore 2; da Zell am Ziller, ore 3.30; da Ramsberg, ore 2.30-3. Traversate: a Mayrhofen, ore 3; al rif. Brandberger Kolmhaus, ore 2.30-3. Cime: Gerlossteinwand, 2166 m, ore 1.30 (facile); Hochfeld, 2350 m, ore 2 (facile).

Grawandhütte (Rifugio), 1636 m (C 8), privato, CAP: 6295 Ginzling, aperto in estate. Accesso: dall'albergo Breitlahner, ore 1.30. Traversata: al rif. Alpenrosehütte, 45 min.

Greizerhütte (Rifugio), 2227 m (E 7, F 19), Alpenverein, CAP: 6290 Mayrhofen, aperto in estate. Accesso: da Ginzling, ore 4. Traversate: al rif. Berliner Hütte, per la forcella Nördliche Mörchenscharte, ore 5.30; al rif. Grüne-Wand-Hütte per la forcella Lapenscharte, ore 4; al rif. Kasseler Hütte, ore 5. Cime: Großer Löffler, 3378 m, ore 3.30 (difficoltà media); Schwarzenstein, 3369 m, ore 4 (difficoltà media).

Grüne-Wand-Hütte (Rifugio), 1436 m (G 18), privato, CAP: 6290 Mayrhofen, aperto in estate. Accesso: da Mayrhofen, ore 4 o con il taxi dall'Europahaus di Mayrhofen; dall'albergo alpino Alpengasthof Wasserfall, ore 2. Traversate: al rif. Kasseler Hütte, ore 2; al rif. Greizerhütte per la forcella Lapenscharte, ore 6.

Häusling-Alpengasthof (Albergo alpino), 1053 m (GH 15), privato, CAP: 6290 Mayrhofen, aperto tutto l'anno. Accesso: da Mayrhofen, ore 2.30; raggiungibile anche in auto (strada a pedaggio - traffico limitato) o in autobus. Traversata: all'albergo In der Au, ore 1.30; accessibile anche in macchina o autobus.

Hochferner, Bivacco (Günther Messner, Bivacco), 2429 m (B 9), Alpenverein, accessibile tutto l'anno. Accesso: da S. Giacomo di Vizze, ore 4; da Sasso/Stein, ore 3; dal 5° tornante della strada per il passo di Vizze, ore 1.

Höllensteinhütte (Rifugio), 1710 m (B 4), privato, CAP: 6293 Lanersbach, aperto in estate. Accesso: dalla fermata autobus di Juns (circa 2 km a sud di Lanersbach), ore 1.30.

In der Au (Albergo), 1265 m (H 16), privato, CAP: 6290 Mayrhofen, aperto tutto l'anno. Accesso: da Mayrhofen, ore 4; anche in auto (strada a pedaggio - traffico limitato) o in autobus. Traversata: a Bärenbad, 45 min.

Innerböden (Albergo), 1301 m (D 5), privato, CAP: 6295 Ginzling, aperto tutto l'anno. Accesso: da Ginzling, ore 1.

Kasseler Hütte (Rifugio), 2178 m (G 18), Alpenverein, CAP: 6290 Mayrhofen, aperto in estate. Accessi: da Mayrhofen, ore 6; dal rif. Grüne-Wand-Hütte, ore 2 (fin lì in taxi dall'Europahaus di Mayrhofen). Traversate: alta via per la Lapenscharte al rif. Greizerhütte, ore 4-5; al rif. Edelhütte sul sentiero Siebenschneidensteig, ore 9-10. Cime: Grüne-Wand-Spitze, 2946 m, ore 2.30; Wollbachspitze, 3209 m, ore 3.

Klaushof (Albergo), 1022 m (G 15), privato, CAP: 6290 Mayrhofen, aperto tutto l'anno. Accesso: da Mayrhofen, ore 2; accessibile anche in auto (strada a pedaggio - traffico limitato) o in autobus. Traversata: a Häusling, 30 min.

Lacknerbrunn (Albergo alpino), 1006 m (D 3), privato, CAP: 6290 Mayrhofen, aperto tutto l'anno. Accesso: da Mayrhofen, ore 1.30, accesso anche in macchina (strada a pedaggio) o in taxi dall'Europahaus di Mayrhofen. Traversate: all'albergo alpino Wasserfall, 45 min.; al rif. Edelhütte, ore 4.

Max-Hütte (Rifugio), 1445 m (D 6), privato, CAP: 6292 Finkenberg, aperto in estate. Accesso: da Ginzling, ore 1.30. Traversata: al rif. Berliner Hütte per la forcella Melkerscharte, ore 7.

Olpererhütte (Rifugio), 2388 m (B 7), Alpenverein, CAP: 6295 Ginzling, aperto in estate. Accesso: dal bacino artificiale Schlegeisspeicher (fin lì in auto, strada a pedaggio, o in autobus), ore 1.30. Traversate: al rif. Friesenberghaus, ore 2; al rif. Geraer Hütte per la Alpeiner Scharte, ore 4. Cime: Olperer, 3476 m, ore 3 (solo per esperti); Gefrorene-Wand-Spitzen, 3288 m, ore 3.30 (solo per esperti).

Passo di Vizze, Rifugio (Pfitscher-Joch-Haus), 2275 m (A 9), privato, CAP: I-39040 S. Giacomo di Vizze, aperto in estate. Accessi: fino al rifugio; da Sasso/Stein, ore 1.15; da S. Giacomo di Vizze ore 1.45.; dal bacino artificiale Schlegeisspeicher, ore 2. Traversate: al rif. Landshuter Europahütte, ore 3.30; al rif. Geraer Hütte, ore 5; al rif. Furtschaglhaus, ore 5. Cime: Schrammacher, 3410 m, ore 4 (solo per esperti); Hohe Wand-Spitze, 3289 m, ore 4 (difficile).

Plauener Hütte (Rifugio), 2364 m (K 16), Alpenverein, CAP: 6283 Hippach, aperto in estate. Accesso: da Mayrhofen, ore 7.30-8; accessibile anche in auto (strada a pedaggio - traffico limitato) o in autobus fino a Bärenbad, da lì ore 2. Traversata: al rif. Richterhütte per la forcella Gamsscharte, ore 3. Cima: Richterspitze, 3052 m, ore 2.30 (difficoltà media).

Richterhütte (Rifugio), 2367 m (K 16), Alpenverein, CAP: 5743 Krimml, aperto in estate. Accessi: dal rif. Krimmler Tauernhaus, ore 2.30; da Krimml, ore 5-6. Traversate: al rif. Plauener Hütte, ore 3; al rif. Zittauer Hütte, ore 3.30; al rif. Tridentina (Birnlückenhütte), ore 7.15. Cime: Windbachtalkogel, 2843 m, ore 1.30 (facile); Richterspitze, 3052 m, ore 2.30 (difficoltà media).

Rosshag, 1096 m (C 6), albergo privato, CAP: 6295 Ginzling, aperto tutto l'anno. Accesso: da Ginzling, ore 1 oppure anche in macchina. Traversata: all'albergo Breitlahner, ore 1.30 oppure anche in macchina.

Spannagelhaus (Rifugio), 2531 m (A 6), Österreichischer Touristenclub, CAP: 6294 Hintertux, aperto in estate e inverno. A pochi minuti dal rifugio si trova la grotta Spannagelhöhle! Accesso: da Hintertux, ore 3.30 oppure con la funivia. Traversate: al rif. Tuxer-Joch-Haus, ore 1.30; al rif. Friesenberghaus per la Friesenbergscharte, ore 3.30. Nei pressi del rifugio si trova una palestra di roccia dove esperte guide insegnano le regole fondamentali dell'alpinismo, sicurezza di passo, tecnica delle funi, corretta arrampicata, ecc.

Stein (Albergo), 1555 m (A 10), privato, CAP: I-39040 San Giacomo di Vizze, aperto tutto l'anno. Accesso: da San Giacomo di Vizze, ore 1, accessibile anche in macchina. Traversata: al rif. Venna alla Gerla, attraverso il passo di Vizze, ore 4.45

Steinerkogl (Albergo alpino), 1270 m (E 2, F 14), privato, CAP: 6290 Mayrhofen, aperto tutto l'anno. Accessi: da Mayrhofen, ore 1.30; da Brandberg, 45 min. Traversate: al rif. Brandberger Kolmhaus, ore 2; all'albergo alpino Gerlosstein, ore 2.30.

Stilluphaus (Rifugio), 1192 m (FG 17), privato, CAP: 6290 Mayrhofen, aperto in estate. Accesso: da Mayrhofen, ore 3 o in taxi dall'Europahaus di Mayrhofen; dall'albergo alpino Wasserfall, ore 1. Traversata: al rif. Grüne-Wand-Hütte, ore 1.

Tuxer-Joch-Haus (Rifugio), 2310 m (A 5), Österreichischer Touristenclub, CAP: 6294 Hintertux, aperto in estate. Accessi: da Hintertux, ore 2.30; dalla stazione a monte della funivia Sommerbergalm, 45 min.; da Kasern nella Schmirntal, ore 2. Traversate: al rif. Spannagelhaus, ore 2; al rif. Geraer Hütte per la Kleegrubenscharte, ore 4.30. Cime: Hornspitze, 2650 m, ore 3 (solo per esperti); Frauenwand, 2541 m, ore 1 (facile).

Vittorio Veneto, Rifugio (Schwarzensteinhütte), 2922 m (E 8), CAI, CAP: I-39030 Luttago, aperto in estate. Accesso: da Luttago, ore 5.30. Cima: Sasso Nero/Schwarzenstein, 3369 m, ore 1.30 (difficoltà media).

Wasserfall (Albergo alpino), 1120 m (E 4, F 16), nella Stillupgrund, privato, CAP: 6290 Mayrhofen, aperto in estate. Accesso: da Mayrhofen, ore 2, anche con la macchina (strada a pedaggio) o in taxi dall'Europahaus di Mayrhofen. Traversata: per il rif. Stilluphaus al rif. Grüne-Wand-Hütte, ore 2.

Wiesenhof (Albergo), 1058 m (E 3, F 15), privato, CAP: 6290 Mayrhofen, aperto tutto l'anno. Accesso: da Mayrhofen, ore 1.30 oppure anche in macchina.

Zittauer Hütte (Rifugio), 2328 m (K 14), Alpenverein, CAP: 5743 Krimml, aperto in estate. Accessi: dalla trattoria Finkau, ore 3: da Gerlos, ore 5; dal passo Gerlos, ore 5. Traversate: al rif. Krimmler Tauernhaus, ore 3; al rif. Richterhütte, ore 3.30. Cime: Rosskopf, 2845 m, ore 1.30 (facile); Reichenspitze, 3303 m, ore 4 (difficile).

ZILLERTAL ACTIVCARD

La Zillertal Activcard per l'estate 2009 vale nella Zillertal per tutte le funivie (controllare gli orari d'apertura stagionale!), le piscine all'aperto (a Fügen, Stumm, Zell, Hippach, Mayrhofen e Finkenberg), il Planetarium a Königsleiten e la maggior parte dei mezzi pubblici della zona (informazioni più dettagliate nell'opuscolo Zillertal Activcard). Non comprendono invece il pedaggio! Nell'estate del 2009 la Zillertal Activcard Vi assicura la riduzione del 10% presso molti gestori nella Zillertal e dintorni. La Zillertal Activcard è a disposizione presso tutte le stazioni delle funivie, le stazioni ferroviarie (orari vendita limitati!) di Jenbach, Zell e Mayrhofen, negli Uffici turistici di Fügen, Uderns, Kaltenbach, Zell im Zillertal, Königsleiten, Hippach, Mayrhofen, Tux e presso la Zillertal Tourismus GmbH a Schlitters. Non è trasferibile ed è valida solo con un documento di riconoscimento (da presentare all'acquisto) e con il nome dell'utilitario riportato sulla Card!

Attenzione: Con la Zillertal Activcard ogni giorno si può acquisire gratis un biglietto di andata ed uno di ritorno con una funivia a Vostra scelta (andata e ritorno sono possibili anche con due funivie diverse) e ogni giorno godete di un'entrata libera in una piscina all'aperto. La Zillertal Activcard non è in vendita per chi pratica il parapendio! La Zillertal Activcard è in vendita per 6, 9 o 12 giorni consecutivi. Riduzioni per bambini: bambini nati dal 2003 in poi gratis; bambini nati tra il 1994 ed il 2002 pagano la tariffa bambini. Carta famiglia: acquistando due biglietti per adulti tutti i bimbi (nati entro la fine del 1994) viaggiano gratis. È necessario un documento di riconoscimento!

Informazioni: Zillertal Tourismus GmbH, Bundesstraße 27 d, 6262 Schlitters Tel. 05288/87187 • Fax 87187-1 • www.zillertal.at • info@zillertal.at

---

Fonti informative su aree vietate o riserve speciali:
Nello sforzo di armonizzare sinergeticamente gli interessi dei cacciatori e delle guardie forestali con quelli degli appassionati della montagna, sia a piedi che in rampichino, il Club alpino austriaco (www.alpenverein.or.at/naturschutz (Bergsport und Umwelt), telefono + +43/(0)512/59547) ha realizzato una banca dati che riporta tutte le zone di caccia, le riserve naturali, le aree sotto particolare tutela faunistica e floreale o altro e le zone militari presenti sul territorio austriaco, come anche le più importanti aree di rilevante interesse paesaggistico e ambientale.
La ditta KOMPASS-Karten GmbH ringrazia l'Alpenverein austriaco per le informazioni pervenute per l'aggiornamento della presente carta KOMPASS.

---

*Segnale di soccorso alpino: mandare **per sei volte** in un minuto, a intervalli regolari, un segnale visibile o udibile, poi fare una pausa di un minuto. Si ripete finché non si riceve risposta.*

*Risposta: entro un minuto viene mandato **per tre volte**, a intervalli regolari, un segnale visibile o udibile.*

Ringraziamo le Associazioni turistiche e l'Alpenverein che hanno dato il loro valido contributo all'aggiornamento della presente guida KOMPASS mettendo inoltre a disposizione anche materiale fotografico.

Descrizione delle località

Troverete i numeri di telefono e di fax delle Associazioni Turistiche e degli uffici comunali a pag. 77.

BRANDBERG   E 2/F 14

Comune, Distretto di Schwaz, abitanti: 350, altezza s.l.m.: 1082 m, CAP: 6290. **Informazioni:** Gemeindeamt (Municipio). **Stazione ferroviaria:** Mayrhofen (6 km). **Collegamento autobus:** con Mayrhofen.

Alto sulla conca Zillergrund si adagia su un ripido pendio montuoso il piccolo centro di villeggiatura di Brandberg. Solo agli inizi del XIX sec. la località di Mayrhofen venne divisa dal comune principale di „Pramberg" e divenne comune autonomo. Con le sue frazioni, i masi singoli, le malghe ed i pascoli sul pendio soleggiato del „Pramberg" o „Brandberg" e nella lunga conca Zillergrund divenne un vero comune montano che si è trasformato ultimamente in una meta privilegiata dal turismo.

Con i suoi 156 km^2 di superficie Brandberg è uno dei Comuni più vasti della Zillertal, giace in una posizione climaticamente favorevole ed è un punto di partenza ideale per escursioni nella zona. Il paesaggio naturale e quello coltivato offrono agli amanti della natura svariate possibilità per il tempo libero. La località è accessibile su una larga strada ed offre anche sufficienti posti di parcheggio.

Curiosità del luogo e dintorni

Nella **parrocchiale neoclassica della S. Croce** su un altare laterale si trova un interessante Madonna tardogotica; all'esterno un monumento ai caduti; sopra il portale una Mater dolorosa; mosaici; nuova cappella mortuaria 1977/78. – **Fontana del paese** con piccole figure dello scultore Albin Moroder di Mayrhofen. – Dell'artista sono anche **le stazioni della Via Crucis** alla cappella di Brandberg. – **Parco naturale Zillertaler Alpen.**

Passeggiate ed escursioni

All'albergo alpino Steinerkogl, 1270 m, per Emberg, 45 min. – Al rif. Brandberger Kolmhaus, 1845 m, ore 2 ca. e al Brandberger Kolm, 2700 m, totale ore 4.30. – All'albergo alpino Gerlosstein, 1620 m, per la Labergalm e la Kotahornalm, ore 3.30. – Nella Zillergrund per la trattoria Klaushof, 1022 m, ore 1 ca., si prosegue all'albergo Häusling, totale ore 1.30 ca., e oltre fino a In der Au, 1265 m, totale ore 3, o anche fino a Bärenbad, 1450 m, totale ore 4. Questo percorso è accessibile anche in auto (strada a pedaggio, traffico limitato!) o in autobus. – Da Bärenbad al bacino artificiale Zillergründl, ca. ore 1.30. – Al rif. Plauener Hütte, 2364 m, da Bärenbad, ore 2. – Al ristorante Adlerblick,

Giovani marmotte/Murmeltierjunge/Young marmots

1900 m, 45 min. da Bärenbad o con il servizio navetta. – Alla malga Kainzenhüttenalm, 1550 m, nel Sundergrund, da In der Au ca. ore 1.30. – Alla Bodenalm, 1670 m, da Häusling, ore 1.30.

Comune, Distretto di Schwaz, abitanti: 1520, altezza s.l.m.: 839 m, CAP: 6292. **Informazioni:** Tourismusverband (Associazione Turistica) Tux - Finkenberg. **Stazione ferroviaria:** Mayrhofen (3 km). **Collegamento autobus:** con Mayrhofen e alla stazione a valle degli impianti di risalita Hintertuxer Gletscherbahnen a Hintertux. **Impianti di risalita:** Finkenberger Almbahnen, varie seggiovie e sciovie nella zona del Penkenjoch.

La località turistica sia invernale che estiva si adagia su una terrazza soleggiata alta sulla profonda forra di foce del torrente Tux. Finkenberg è il secondo maggior comune della Zillertal per estensione, anche se il territorio è prevalentemente incolto. Esso non comprende solo i masi e le frazioni in parte già menzionati agli inizi del XIV sec., che sul versante soleggiato della valle Tuxer Tal inferiore salgono fino a quasi 1400 m, e le alte malghe e cascine, ma anche i territori sulla riva ovest del torrente Zemm fino alla chiusa delle valli Zamser e Schlegeisgrund e fino all'odierno confine di stato verso sud. Nel 1991 questo incredibile scenario alpino venne dichiarato „zona di riposo" (ora parco naturale Zillertaler Alpen) dalla dieta regionale tirolese. La tutela di questa zona quindi vieta di costruirvi in futuro altre sciovie o strade pubbliche.

Finkenberg raggiunse una certa fama allorché nel 1980 durante le olimpiadi Leonhard Stock vinse la medaglia d'oro nella discesa libera e quindi anche il titolo mondiale.

Curiosità del luogo e dintorni
Parrocchiale di S. Leonardo, costruita nel 1720, ampliata nel XIX sec.; l'arredo interno per gran parte risale al periodo di costruzione. – Il **Teufelsbrücke** (ponte del diavolo) sulla profonda forra del torrente Tux è una costruzione in legno del 1876. – La piccola **cascata** sopra il paese. – **Percorso didattico naturalistico „Glocke".** – **Itinerario didattico palustre** al **Penkenjoch.**

Passeggiate ed escursioni
Dalla chiesa passando per lo Sporer, la cascata ed il sentiero boschivo e ritorno, ore 1. – A Stein (albergo Gletscherblick), salita dalla chiesa e discesa per Persal ed il ponte Teufelsbrücke, da lì di ritorno per il sentiero Klammweg, ore 2. – Escursione circolare dalla chiesa per il ponte Teufelsbrücke all'albergo Schöne Aussicht, poi oltre, lungo il bacino artificiale di raccolta „Dornau", oltrepassando l'albergo Martins Wirtshaus allo Jochberg, sulla strada per la pensione Forellenhof alla pensione Hochsteg. Da lì al margine della forra si ritorna al ponte del diavolo e quindi al paese, totale ore 2.30. – All'albergo Astegg, 1176 m, superando Stein, ore 1; discesa verso Mayrhofen sul Mariensteig dal quale si passa, ad ovest del torrente Zemm, sul sentiero prativo che riconduce a Finkenberg, ca. ore 2. – A Innerberg (fermata autobus) seguendo la strada per Persal, 45 min.; superando il ponte Rosengarten a Gschwendt e Brunnhaus e ritorno per il Teufelsbrücke oppure si supera il ponticello e passando per la piscina si arriva alla strada presso Persal, ore 2.30-3. – A Vorderlanersbach attraverso Altenstall, Katzenmoos, Möser e Außerrettenbach, ore 3. – Al rif. Gschößwandhaus, 1762 m, per l'albergo Astegg, ore 3. – Al rif. Penkenhaus, 1814 m, ore 3; più oltre al rif. Penkenjochhaus, 2095 m, stazione a monte dell'impianto di risalita Finkenberger Almbahn, 45 min. – Al rif. Gamshütte, 1921 m, percorrendo il sentiero Hermann-Hecht-Weg, ore 3. – All'albergo Innerböden, 1301 m, e alla Oberbödenalm, 1500 m, da Ginzling, ore 2. – Al rif. Max-Hütte, 1445 m, da Ginzling, ore 1.30. – Al rif. Greizerhütte, 2227 m, da Ginzling attraverso la Floitengrund, ca. ore 3.15. – All'albergo Breitlahner, 1256 m, da Ginzling, ore 1.30-2. – Al rif. Berliner Hütte, 2042 m, dall'albergo Breitlahner attraverso la Zemmgrund per i rifugi Grawandhütte e Alpenrosehütte, ore 2.30. – Al rif. Dominikushütte, 1805 m, da Ginzling, ore 4.30. – Al rif. Furtschaglhaus, 2295 m, dal rif. Dominikushütte attraverso lo Zamsgatterl e sull'alta via Berliner Höhenweg, poi lungo il lago artificiale Schlegeisspeicher e al rifugio, ore 3. – Al rif. Passo di Vizze, 2275 m, dal rif. Dominikushütte attraverso lo Zamsgatterl e nella Zamser Grund al passo di Vizze e al rifugio, ore 2. – Al rif. Olpererhütte, 2388 m, dal rif. Dominikushütte, prima per circa 10 minuti lun-

go il lago artificiale fino alla biforcazione (sentiero n. 502) a destra per il rifugio, ore 1. – Al rif. Friesenberghaus, 2498 m, prima fino al rif. Olpererhütte e da lì sull'alta via Berliner Höhenweg (sentiero n. 526) passando per il lago Friesenberg, al rifugio, ore 3 o direttamente dal bacino artificiale al rifugio (sentiero n. 532), ore 2.

GERLOS

I 12

Comune, Distretto di Schwaz, abitanti: 800, altezza s.l.m.: 1245 m, CAP: 6281. **Informazioni:** Tourismusverband (Associazione Turistica) Gerlos - Zell. **Stazione ferroviaria:** Zell am Ziller (18 km). **Collegamento autobus:** con Zell am Ziller, Mayrhofen e Wald im Pinzgau. **Impianti di risalita:** Numerose seggiovie e sciovie.

Con la costruzione della statale per il passo Gerlos (1531 m) e del bacino artificiale Durlaßboden, con la realizzazione delle piste da sci e di moderne attrezzature turistiche l'era della tecnica ha raggiunto anche la solitaria valle di Gerlos. Ma poco distante dalla strada regna ancora la quiete dei vasti alpeggi e delle cime di ogni tipo di difficoltà. Nel simpatico abitato longitudinalmente ognuno si troverà a proprio agio.

Curiosità del luogo e dintorni

La **parrocchiale dei SS. Leonardo e Lamberto** fu edificata tra il 1730-1735 da Hans Holzmeister di Hippach; i dipinti sul soffitto sono opera di Josef Michael Schmutzer di Wessobrunn; gli altari del periodo di costruzione furono in parte rinnovati, sull'altar maggiore statua della Madonna di Josef Bachlechner, 1911. – Il **bacino artificiale di Durlaßboden** allo sbocco della valle Wildgerlostal nella valle principale Gerlostal.

Passeggiate ed escursioni

Per la Schönachtal: alla malga Stinkmoosalm, 1348 m, ca. 45 min., si prosegue in dolce salita al posto di ristoro Lackenalm, 1400 m, 30 min. – Alla malga Issalm per la Schönachtal e attraverso la Pasteinalm, 1692 m, fino nella conca valliva più interna, ca. ore 3. – A Gmünd attraverso la malga Gerlostalalm, 1756 m, e poi di ritorno sul sentiero boschivo, ore 4 ca. – Nella Wimmertal e fino al rif. Grundhütte, 1685 m, da Gmünd, ca. ore 1.30-2. – Al passo Gerlospass, 1531 m, lungo il sentiero a lunga percorrenza delle Alpi Centrali n. 02 (variante) per le malghe Königsleiten, ore 4. – Sul Schönbichl, 2049 m, da Gerlos passando per la Kreidlschlagalm dapprima sulle larghe propaggini settentrionali della cresta montuosa Schönachkamm; poi lungo queste sulla cupola erbosa molto panoramica, ca. ore 2.30. – Sull'Arbiskogel, 2048 m, direttamente da Gerlos in direzione sud, ore 2.30 (utilizzando la seggiovia Fürstalm-

In balia delle acque/Unterwegs im wilden Wasser
Whitewater river-tripping

bahn che sale alla Fürstalm, 1824 m, si accorcia di ore 1.30); traversata poi alla Kirchspitze, 2312 m, 45 min. (facile); variante per la discesa a Gmünd passando per la malga Kothüttenalm. – Al rif. Brandberger Kolmhaus, 1845 m, dall'albergo Kühle Rast (fermata autobus) per il giogo Brandberger Joch, 2307 m, ca. ore 4. – Sull'Isskogel, 2268 m, attraverso la Ebenfeldaste, 1864 m; approfittando della seggiovia Isskogelbahn, ore 1.30. – Al rif. Zittauer Hütte, 2328 m, per la Wildgerlostal; da Gerlos, ore 6, dalla trattoria Finkau, ore 3.

Comune, Distretto di Schwaz, abitanti: 460, altezza s.l.m.: 1100 m, CAP: 6280. **Informazioni**: Tourismusverband (Associazione Turistica) Gerlos-Zell. **Stazione ferroviaria**: Zell am Ziller (5 km). **Collegamento autobus**: per Zell am Ziller.

Il piccolo comune appartenne in passato al Tribunale pupillare di Salisburgo Zell am Ziller ed è rimasto profondamente legato a questo centro fino ai giorni nostri. V. ivi per ulteriori informazioni.

HAINZENBERG

F 12

Comune, Distretto di Schwaz, abitanti: 670, altezza s.l.m.: 944 m, CAP: 6280. **Informazioni**: Gemeindeamt (Municipio). **Stazione ferroviaria**: Zell am Ziller (5 km). **Collegamento autobus**: con Zell am Ziller, Mayrhofen, Gerlos - Wald im Pinzgau. **Impianti di risalita**: Gerlossteinbahn, seggiovia e sciovia Arbiskögerl.

Ai piedi dell'imponente Gerlossteinwand giace la ridente località di Hainzenberg, che confina a sud con il comune di Ramsau im Zillertal, a est con Gerlos, a nord con Gerlosberg e a nord-ovest con Zell am Ziller. È costituita prevalentemente da frazioni sparse. Il centro del comune è ad Hainzenberg, dove si trovano tra l'altro il municipio, la scuola elementare e materna, come anche la stazione a valle della funivia di Gerlosstein.

Sull'Hainzenberg si estrasse oro dagli inizi del XVI sec. fino al XIX sec. Per approfondire questo argomento vale la pena di visitare la miniera d'oro. Oggigiorno gli abitanti vivono di quanto producono e del turismo coadiuvato da alcuni confortevoli esercizi alberghieri. L'allargamento della strada statale ha portato anche altri vantaggi, come la possibilità di piacevoli gite a Zell am See, al Lofer, a Wörgl, alle celebri cascate di Krimml, al passo Thurn ed alla rinomata località mondana di Kitzbühel.

Curiosità del luogo e dintorni

Nella **casa Unterflörler**, costruita nel 1250, si può visitare un'antica **cappella di minatori**, sotto tutela ambientale. Walter Burgstaller, in volgo Wurzelsepp, esperto mineralogista e scultore del legno, cura questa cappella ed anche una **ricca collezione di minerali** aperta al pubblico. – Nelle vicinanze il **caseificio**, accessibile al pubblico, con il chiosco ed il **giardino zoologico**. – Da qui hanno inizio le **visite alla miniera d'oro**. Nell'arco di un'ora una guida vi spiegherà le condizioni di lavoro dei minatori, il loro stile di vita e l'ambiente sociale in cui vissero. – Vale la pena di visitare il **santuario di Maria Rast**, che richiama fortemente la cappella di casa Unterflörler. Portone tardogotico e quattro finestre tardogotiche, recentemente restaurate; arredo del XVIII sec.; stucchi e discreti affreschi sul soffitto, di Josef Michael Schmutzer di Wessobrunn, 1741; bell'altar maggiore rococò di Stefan Föger, 1748, con immagini della Madonna in stile barocco; anche il pulpito sembra sia opera di Föger.

Passeggiate ed escursioni

A Zell am Ziller per Maria Rast sul sentiero boschivo, ore 1. – All'albergo alpino Gerlosstein, 1620 m, dall'ultimo grande tornante della strada statale, circa ore 2.30 oppure dall'albergo Ötschenwirt, ore 2. L'albergo alpino Gerlosstein è raggiungibile anche con la funivia Gerlosstein.

HIPPACH

F 12-13

Comune, Distretto di Schwaz, abitanti: 1380, altezza s.l.m.: 608 m, CAP: 6283. **Informazioni**: Tourismusverband (Associazione Turistica) Hippach - Ramsau - Schwendau. **Stazione ferroviaria**: Ramsau-Hippach. **Collegamento autobus**: con Jenbach, Mayrhofen, Gerlos - Wald im Pinzgau. **Impianti di risalita**: v. Mayrhofen.

La bella località di Hippach è il centro dei comuni turistici che si estendono sul versante ovest della Zillertal superiore ai piedi dello Schwendberg fortemente insediato. La località venne menzionata per la prima volta in atti della metà del XIII sec., ma sicuramente la chiesa e l'insediamento sono molto più antichi. Il toponimo è di origine germanica e si riferisce alla posizione vicina all'ormai domato torrente che ha creato quel cono di deiezione ben visibile tra Hippach e Schwendau. Già verso la fine del XVII sec. Hippach divenne famosa come „Badl", in ted. bagni, per la sua sorgente curativa. Deve il suo sviluppo quale moderno centro turistico non solo alla sua posizione soleggiata, l'ottima posizione di transito e la curata ospitalità, ma anche a numerose personalità del luogo che si sono profilate nel campo della musica, delle belle arti, dello studio e della vita pubblica.

Curiosità del luogo e dintorni

La **chiesa dei SS. Ingenuino ed Albuino** originariamente gotica, fu ristrutturata e barocchizzata dopo il terremoto del 1699. Del periodo gotico sono rimasti il portale spostato nel transetto est e il campanile sul lato meridionale. Le stuccature sono della fine del XVII sec.; i dipinti sul soffitto centrale sono del tardo XIX sec.; gli affreschi laterali sono di Josef Michael Schmutzer di Wessobrunn, 1746; un dipinto laterale è dell'artista locale Matthäus Schiestl, 1914; le statue degli altari laterali sono di quest'ultimo artista e di Johann Sporer; le statue sull'altar maggiore sono in stile barocco. – Particolarmente consigliabile è un viaggio per la **Zillertaler Höhenstraße** (strada panoramica a pedaggio) dalla quale si possono intraprendere anche belle escursioni. – **Tre tigli** sono sotto tutela ambientale. – A **Laimach** si consiglia di visitare il **museo Strasser Häusl**. L'edificio del XVIII, completamente in legno, ben conservato e sotto tutela ambientale, fu l'abitazione dei fratelli Strasser che portarono nel mondo la nota melodia della canzone natalizia „Astro del Ciel" (Stille Nacht, heilige Nacht).

Passeggiate ed escursioni

A Mayrhofen o attraverso il ponte sullo Ziller e lungo la riva orientale oppure ad ovest per Stockach, Mühlbach e Burgstallschrofen, ore 1. – A Zell am Ziller per la passeggiata Ziller-Promenade sulla riva orientale oppure sulla strada per Laimach e Zellbergeben, ca. ore 1. – Alle cascate Laimacher e Talbach seguendo il sentiero Prof.-Dr.-Rieser. Il sentiero segnato per le cascate devia dal tornante stradale; si ritorna per Laimach, ore 2. – Alla cascata Keiler e ritorno per Schwendau, ore 2 ca. – All'albergo Mösl, ore 2.30. – Al rif. Gschößwandhaus, 1762 m, dall'albergo Mösl, ore 1.30. – Al rif. Rastkogelhütte, 2117 m, dall'albergo Mösl, ore 2.

MAYRHOFEN   E 2/F 14

Comune, Distretto di Schwaz, abitanti: 3980, altezza s.l.m.: 633 m, CAP: 6290. **Informazioni:** Tourismusverband (Associazione Turistica) Mayrhofen. **Stazione ferroviaria:** Mayrhofen. **Collegamento autobus:** con Jenbach, la stazione a valle degli impianti di risalita Hintertuxer Gletscherbahnen a Hintertux, Brandberg, Ginzling, Gerlos - Wald im Pinzgau, con il ristorante Schlegeis al bacino artificiale Schlegeisspeicher, con l'albergo Wasserfall al bacino artificiale Stillup e con l'albergo Bärenbad ed inoltre con il bacino artificiale Zillergründl. Nella stagione invernale servizio navetta gratuito alle funivie. **Impianti di risalita:** funivie, seggiovie e sciovie.

Mayrhofen e la più antica e rinomata località turistica della regione. È situata nella conca valliva della Zillertal superiore e circondata dal magnifico scenario del parco naturale delle Zillertaler Alpen.

Qui staziona il formaggio/Hier reift der Käse/Where the cheese matures

Vordere Stangenspitze, 3127 m, e/und/and Hintere Stangenspitze, 3225 m

Fino al 1801 Mayrhofen fece parte del comune di Brandberg. La località rurale era raggiungibile da sud solo su impervie mulattiere e da nord per una strada malmessa.
Oggi invece ognuno trova quello che cerca. Mayrhofen è diventato il centro turistico della valle per eccellenza, ma ha saputo mantenere integro il suo carattere nonostante il suo continuo sviluppo e la sua modernizzazione.

Curiosità del luogo e dintorni

Negli abitati di Haus e Brandberg si possono ammirare antichi **masi**, come ad es. il maso zum Griena, di ben oltre 400 anni, che oggi ospita una locanda caratteristica, oppure il Gratzerhaus, della seconda metà del XVII sec. Gli appassionati di arte contemporanea resteranno affascinati dalla Karg Haus nella Scheulingstraße, la cui facciata è stata realizzata dall'artista tirolese Patrizia Karg. – Anche la **parrocchiale „Unsere Liebe Frau"** a Mayrhofen, con l'affresco sul soffitto della „rosa di Gerico", di Max Weiler, è un'ulteriore attrazione per gli amanti dell'arte. – Tutto quanto c'è da sapere sul formaggio, sulla vita in malga e le tradizioni della popolazione si può trovare nell'**Erlebnis Sennerei Zillertal**, dove su una superficie di 6.000 m² dal 2000 si può seguire dettaglio per dettaglio la lavorazione del latte e del formaggio. – Il **grande rilievo delle Alpi Zillertaler** nell'**Europahaus** è di Fritz Ebster. Permette una vasta panoramica della zona con il parco naturale e serve anche a progettare gite ed escursioni. – **Parco naturale Zillertaler Alpen.**

Passeggiate ed escursioni

Alla cappella di pellegrinaggio sul Burgschrofen dalla piazza inferiore del paese, 30 min. – A Ramsau per la frazione di Durst e lungo il bosco attraverso Laubichl, Hollenzen, Eckartau, ore 1. – A Zimmereben, dal Mariensteig dopo ca. 20 min. di salita il sentiero devia in direzione nord, dalla piazza inferiore del paese, circa ore 1. – All'albergo Zillergrund sulla carrozzabile, 30 min.; di ritorno sul sentiero che devia a sinistra vicino al ponte e conduce attraverso Kumbichl, 45 min. – Al rif. Edelhütte, 2238 m, o con la funivia Ahornbahn all'Hahnpfalz e da lì in ore 1 al rifugio o da Mayrhofen per l'albergo Alpenrose e la Fellenbergalm, ore 4.30-5. – Al piccolo santuario di Brandberg attraverso il bosco Scheuling, 45 min. – Da qui poi a destra sulla carrozzabile fino a Brandberg, 45 min. – A Zell am Ziller lungo la passeggiata Ziller-Promenade sulla riva est del torrente, ore 2. – All'albergo Astegg lungo il sentiero Mariensteig, ca. ore 2; da lì discesa a Finkenberg, 45 min. e di ritorno per il sentiero prativo, ca. ore 1. – All'albergo Lacknerbrunn, 1006 m, attraverso gli abitati di Haus e Schmelzhütten, con la centrale elettrica Mayrhofen, dove inizia il romantico sentiero attraverso la gola Stillupklamm che sale lungo cascate ed infine ripido per il bosco e poco sotto la biforcazione per il Wiesenhof raggiunge la carrozzabile, ca. ore 1.30. – Per il Wiesenhof, 1058 m, si devia a sinistra presso l'albergo Brücke e passando per i bei masi di Kumbichl si arriva ad una carrareccia che a destra comodamente conduce in alto oppure, arrivati al bivio, si continua ancora diritti sul sentiero per l'„Alpenrose" dal quale ben presto un sentiero boschivo devia a destra, ca. ore 1.30. – Al rif. Penkenhaus, 1814 m, con la cabinovia Penkenbahn alla stazione a monte e alla meta e ritorno per l'albergo Astegg, ore 3.30. – Sul Rastkogel, 2762 m, con la cabinovia Penkenbahn alla stazione a monte e attraverso la Wanglalm e la Wanglspitz, 2420 m, si sale alla vetta. Si ritorna per lo stesso sentiero, ore 6. – Sulla Ahornspitze, 2973 m, con la funivia Ahornbahn al Hahnpfalz e passando per il rif. Edelhütte, 2238 m, alla cima, ore 3.30. – Al rif. Kasseler Hütte, 2178 m, dall'albergo Wasserfall, presso il bacino artificiale Stillup, sul sentiero n. 515 al rif. Grüne-Wand-Hütte, 1436 m, e al rifugio, ore 2.30. – Ulteriori proposte escursionistiche, soprattutto in alta montagna, sono riportate ai capitoli Alte Vie e Elenco degli alberghi e dei rifugi alpini.

RAMSAU im Zillertal
E 1/F 13

Comune, distretto di Schwaz, abitanti: 1580, altezza s.l.m.: 604, CAP: 6284. **Informazioni**: Tourismusverband (Associazione Turistica) Hippach - Ramsau - Schwendau. **Stazione ferroviaria**: Ramsau-Hippach. **Collegamento autobus**: Jenbach, Mayrhofen, Zell am Ziller, Gerlos - Wald im Pinzgau. **Impianti di risalita**: Seggiovie e sciovie.

Gli abitati compresi nel Comune di Ramsau si adagiano sui pendii del Ramsberg che nonostante il forte disboscamento è ancora molto boschivo, o ai piedi di questo al limite orien-

Ramsjoch

tale del fondovalle della Zillertal superiore. Per il turismo Ramsau è associato ad Hippach. La seggiovia di Ramsberg e numerosi e comodi sentieri conducono l'escursionista in una zona oltremodo interessante ad alta quota.

Curiosità del luogo e dintorni

La **parrocchiale dell'Addolorata**, in ted. zu den Sieben Schmerzen Mariens, del tardo classicismo: l'altar maggiore è allestito tra l'altro con statue dei SS. Isidoro e Notburga del 1770.
– A **Oberbichl** lo **Studio Alte Mühle**, di Max Hochmuth (volgo Wurzelmax), che guadagna da vivere per sè e la numerosa famiglia producendosi come pittore, intagliatore, musicista, mineralogista e commerciante in minerali e non ultimo come „autentico Zillertaler".

Passeggiate ed escursioni

A Zell am Ziller lungo la passeggiata Ziller-Promenade, 50 minuti oppure ai piedi del Ramsberg per l'abitato di Schweiber ed infine percorrendo la strada, ore 1. – A Mayrhofen per la passeggiata Ziller-Promenade oppure per gli abitati di Unterbichl e Oberbichl, Eckartau e Hollenzen e in parte per il bosco di tigli Lindenwald, ore 1. – A Mayrhofen per la stazione a monte della seggiovia Ramsberglift, la Kotahornalm e l'albergo alpino Steinerkogl, 1270 m, ore 4.30-5. – Alla stazione intermedia della seggiovia, da Ramsau, per il posto di ristoro Waldheim, ore 1. – All'albergo alpino Gerlosstein, 1620 m, passando per la stazione a monte della seggiovia Ramsberglift, ore 2.

ROHRBERG	G 11

Comune, Distretto di Schwaz, abitanti: 520, altezza s.l.m.: ca. 1000 m, CAP: 6280. **Informazioni:** Tourismusverband (Associazione Turistica) Zell - Gerlos. **Stazione ferroviaria:** Zell am Ziller, da Rohr (1,5 km). Per il resto v. Zell am Ziller.

La piccola località montana è composta prevalentemente da frazioni sparse sorte da abitati nel corso della bonifica effettuata nel medioevo.

Passeggiate ed escursioni: v. Zell am Ziller.

SCHWENDAU	E 1/F 13

Comune, Distretto di Schwaz, abitanti: 1550, altezza s.l.m.: 620 m, CAP: 6283. **Informazioni:** Tourismusverband (Associazione Turistica) Hippach - Ramsau - Schwendau. **Stazione ferroviaria:** Hippach (ca. 0,2 km). **Collegamento autobus:** v. Hippach. **Impianti di risalita:** v. Mayrhofen.

Schwendau sorge al limite della radura valliva soleggiata vicino alla foce del torrente Sidan nella valle principale. I torrenti Sidan e Hoarberg hanno tagliato la tenera fillade quarzifera ed hanno costruito un largo conoide di deiezione attraverso il quale lo Ziller viene spinto verso est. Il toponimo della località viene menzionato per la prima volta attorno al 1200 come Swentouwe nell'Urbarium del convento di Salisburgo e conferma assieme ai toponimi Schwendberg e Stockach il forte lavoro di disboscamento dei primi coloni. Schwendau diede i natali al dottore di montagna, il signor Kiendler, deceduto nel 1934, la cui fama giunse fino in Giappone. I suoi singolari metodi di cura vivono ancora nei racconti e qualcuno trova tuttora applicazione pratica.

Curiosità del luogo e dintorni

La **cappella del Redentore crocifisso** al Burgstallschrofen venne costruita nel 1844. – La **cascata Keiler**. – **Forno (Brennhütte)**. – **Mulino Zimmerhäusl**, aperto al pubblico. – **Antichi masi contadini**. – **Cappella**. – **Fontana di Johann Sponring**.

Passeggiate

A Hippach, 30 min. – A Mayrhofen lungo la passeggiata Ziller-Promenade per Mühlbach, Burgstall e Burgstallschrofen, 45 min. – Alla cascata Keiler, ore 1. – All'albergo Zimmereben, da Burgstall, 50 minuti; discesa eventualmente a Mayrhofen o Finkenberg. – A Burgstall seguendo il sentiero nel bosco di Schwendau per Mühlen e poi si ritorna lungo la passeggiata Ziller-Promenade, ore 1.30.

Comune, Distretto di Schwaz, abitanti: 1920, altezza s.l.m.: 1300-3476 m. CAP: 6293. **Informazioni**: Tourismus-verband (Associazione Turistica) Tux - Finkenberg. **Stazione ferroviaria**: Mayrhofen (14 km). **Collegamento autobus**: con Mayrhofen e fino alla stazione a valle degli impianti di risalita Hintertuxer Gletscherbahnen ad Hintertux. **Impianti di risalita**: Hintertuxer Gletscherbahnen (Escursionismo e sci estivo ed invernale con funivie, seggiovie e sciovie), Eggalmbahn (cabinovia a 4 posti).

In fondo alla valle Zillertal, all'altezza di Mayrhofen, 633 m, si diparte la Tuxer Tal. Una strada pittosto curvilinea ma larga, conduce dapprima a Finkenberg, 839 m, indi oltrepassa la forra di Tux con l'imponente ponte Rosengarten e dopo soli 4 km raggiunge il comune di Tux. La località giace tra i 1257 m della frazione di Vorderlanersbach ed i 1493 m di Hintertux. Il rilievo più importante è l'Olperer, 3476 m. Le cinque frazioni del comune di Tux – Hintertux, Madseit, Juns, Lanersbach e Vorderlanersbach – si estendono per 8 km ed offrono ai turisti ed alla popolazione del luogo un ambiente idilliaco per tutto l'arco dell'anno. Fino alla metà del XV sec. Hintertux fece parte della parrocchia di Matrei nella Wipptal. Solo nel 1926 si staccò dal comune di Schmirn e da allora l'antica marca salisburghese di Lanersbach, il capitanato di Lämperbichl e Hintertux fanno parte dell'odierno comune di Tux.

Anche dal punto di vista geologico la località è di un certo interesse, dato che segna il confine geologico tra le Alpi di Tux (scisti argillosi) e la giogaia principale di Tux (gneis granitico). Alla chiusa della valle si eleva il maestoso ghiacciaio di Hintertux che culmina nella montagna dell'Olperer, 3476 m, il rilievo principale della valle. La varietà geomorfologica della zona le conferisce un fascino particolare che entusiasma sia gli escursionisti che gli appassionati di alpinismo. La posizione particolarmente riparata influisce positivamente anche sul clima di Tux, rendendolo più mite, e ciò si manifesta nella vegetazione che rimane verde fino ai margini del ghiacciaio, il che le ha conferito il soprannome di „verde valle del ghiacciaio". La stazione meteorologica di Innsbruck ha elaborato una statistica dei valori medi di Tux nell'arco dell'anno: 1839 ore di sole, 12 giorni di nebbia e 153 giorni di neve nella valle.

In cammino nella Tuxer Tal/Wandern im Tuxer Tal/Hiking in the Tux Valley

Curiosità del luogo e dintorni

Dalle ore 13 alle 16 di tutti i lunedì da giugno a settembre si ha la possibilità di macinare grano al **mulino** di Tux, in località **Juns.** – A **Madseit** la **Mehlerhaus**, maso contadino del XVII sec., abitato fino al 1992, restaurato dal Comune di Tux nel 1999 e aperto al pubblico. Le antiche stubi e la cucina sono visitabili lunedì, ore 14-17. – Nella **Höllensteinhütte** ha

In cammino per il Rastkogel, 2762 m/Auf dem Weg zum Rastkogel, 2762 m
On the trail to Rastkogel, 2762 m

sede il **museo rurale** che offre un'ampia panoramica sulla vita grama dei contadini di montagna e dei taglialegna della zona. – Escursione a valle alle „**tre croci**" di **Hintertux**. – Nei pressi della casa **Spannagelhaus**, 2531 m, a 10 minuti dalla stazione a monte Sektion II delle Hintertuxer Gletscherbahnen, si trova la **grotta Spannagelhöhle**, lunga 4,2 km e profonda fino a 25 m, sotto tutela ambientale dal 1964. È la più grande grotta tirolese con interessanti esempi di fenomeni carsici in alta montagna, dovuti all'erosione dei ghiacciai. Possibilità di visite guidate di un'ora in estate ed in inverno. – **Masi** sotto tutela ambientale, risalenti al XVIII sec. a **Gemais**, a monte di Vorderslanersbach. – Presso **l'antica miniera di magnesite** alla Schrofenalm si trova la **cappella di S. Barbara** con un magnifico affresco del celebre artista contemporaneo Max Weiler. – La malga **Junsalm**, 1984 m, con il posto di ristoro e la **Casera Stoankasern**: da metà giugno a fine settembre si può osservare la lavorazione del latte in burro e formaggio. – **Parrocchiali** e **cappelle** delle varie **frazioni**. – Alla chiusa della valle a Hintertux, sotto la Gefrorene-Wand-Spitze spumeggiano le acque delle **cascate di Tux** che precipitano in profonde conche rocciose. La cosidetta cascata Schraubenwasserfall è sotto tutela ambientale dal 1964. Salendo al Tuxer Joch si può ammirare la cascata Schleierwasserfall.

Passeggiate ed escursioni

250 km di sentieri segnati conducono tra un'interessante flora alpina a laghetti, malghe gestite e cime incantevoli. Escursioni in alta montagna, escursioni didattiche e guidate di ca. 3-7 ore di cammino, tra cui il sentiero delle cascate Wasserfallweg, giro circolare, ca. ore 1.30, ed il sentiero della palude Moorlehrpfad, ore 2. Il sentiero tematico Themenweg, con 9 tabelle informative (clima, acqua, geologia, bosco montano, lavine, larice e peccio, malghe, ghiacciaio e muri a secco), collega in 1 km il centro di Hintertux con il parcheggio degli impianti di risalita Hintertuxer Gletscherbahnen.

Servizio escursionismo: funivie ed un apposito taxi conducono ai punti di partenza per meritevoli escursioni panoramiche, bus gratuito per gli escursionisti. Escursioni su ghiacciaio con attraversamento di crepaccio e arrampicata. Scuola di alpinismo e guide alpine, club di canottaggio, trekking nelle grotte e Flying Fox, Kraxel-Maxel-Camp, ed altro ancora. Escursioni per ogni grado di condizione, dalla semplice passeggiata all'escursione impegnativa in alta montagna; 17 punti di ristoro, risp. rifugi (gestiti da giugno ad ottobre).

Proposte escursionistiche:

Stazione a monte Eggalm, 1948 m, Grüblspitze, 2395 m, lago Torsee, Lanersbach, ore 5. – Stazione a monte Eggalm, 1948 m, Waldhoar, Brandalm, Lanersbach, ore 2.30. – Sommerbergalm, Frauenwand, rif. Tuxer-Joch-Haus, 2310 m, Weitental, Hintertux, ore 4. – Hintertux, Spannagelhaus, 2531 m, a pochi minuti dalla grotta Spannagelhöhle, ritorno in cabinovia, ore 3. – Lämmerbichl, Rastkogel, 2762 m, Vorderlanersbach, ore 6. – Casera Stoankasern, Junsjoch, 2484 m, Juns, ore 5.

Giro da Penken a Lämmerbichl con vista sulla Tuxer Tal
The trail from Penken to Lämmerbichl and back with a view into the Tux Valley
Rundweg Penken – Lämmerbichl mit Blick in das Tuxer Tal

ZELL am Ziller   F 11

Comune, Distretto di Schwaz, abitanti: 1770, altezza s.l.m.: 575 m, CAP: 6280. **Informazioni:** Tourismusverband (Associazione Turistica) Zell - Gerlos. **Stazione ferroviaria:** Zell am Ziller. **Collegamento autobus:** con Jenbach, Mayrhofen, Gerlos – Wald im Pinzgau. **Impianti di risalita:** Cabinovie, seggiovie e sciovie.

Zell am Ziller potè svilupparsi come vivace capoluogo della valle grazie alla sua favorevole posizione a sud della strettoia della valle che divide la Zillertal inferiore da quella superiore. La località si estende sul largo fondovalle sulle rive dello Ziller. Il toponimo fa capire che molto presto qui si trovava una chiesa con convento (cella) i cui possedimenti passarono poi alla colonia. Questa viene già menzionata nel più antico Urbarium dell'arciconvento di Salisburgo (attorno al 1200) come uno dei masi principali del territorio della Zillertal. Zell divenne poi sede di tribunale pupillare e prepositurale e viene indicata fin dal XII sec. quale una delle prime due parrocchie originarie salisburghesi della Zillertal. Ancora oggi è il centro principale della valle poiché è sede delle autorità giudiziarie, decanali e amministrative, di numerose aziende e del terziario. Ogni anno all'inizio di maggio viene tenuta la più antica festa primaverile tirolese, la „Gauderfest", con musica e balli, lotta libera e lotta di animali (montoni) con salami tipici e birra tipica. Quest'ultima viene prodotta appositamente nella birreria del luogo, esistente fin dal 1500, i

Santuario di Maria Rast/Wallfahrtskapelle Maria Rast/Maria Rast Pilgrimage Church

cui proprietari hanno istituito questa festa circa 400 anni fa. Una dimostrazione pratica dell'atavica allegria degli abitanti della Zillertal si può avere in varie occasioni, come nel carnevale, al tempo della transumanza, quando vengono riportate a valle le mucche, o il giorno della sagra paesana, il 15 agosto, festa dell'Assunta.

Curiosità del luogo e dintorni

Della **parrocchiale di S. Vito**, XIV sec., è rimasto solo il campanile ovest gotico a cui venne annesso alla fine del XVIII sec. ad opera di A. Hueber un bell'edificio rococò su progetto di W. Hagenauer; frammenti di affreschi si trovano sul lato ovest dell'atrio; gli affreschi sul soffitto sono del 1500 ca.; il quadro d'altare (S. Vito) e probabilmente anche quelli degli altari laterali sono di Franz Anton Zeiller, 1779; fonte battesimale con gruppo ligneo tardobarocco nell'atrio; al cimitero tomba con pietra araldica di Johann Schoner e consorte, deceduti nel 1451. – **Santuario di Maria Rast, caseificio, miniera d'oro, giardino zoologico**: v. Hainzenberg.

Passeggiate ed escursioni

Vedi anche foglio limitrofo n. 28 „Vorderes Zillertal - Alpbach - Rofan - Wildschönau". Passeggiata circolare dalla piazza del paese, sulla Kraus-Promenade dalla Rohrerstraße alla Gerlosstraße, totale ore 1. – A Mayrhofen lungo la Ziller-Promenade sulla riva est dello Ziller, ore 2; ritorno per Schwendau, Hippach e Laimach. – Al Santuario di Maria Rast per il sentiero n. 7, ore 1.30. – All'albergo alpino Gerlosstein, 1620 m, dalla fermata autobus Ötschenwirt oppure dall'ultimo grande tornante prima di Hainzenberg direttamente per il bosco, ore 2-2.30; da lì si possono effettuare molte escursioni, per esempio alla Gerlossteinwand, 2166 m, ore 1.30-2; all'Arbiskögerl, 1830 m, ore 1; a Mayrhofen per le malghe Kotahorn e Laberg e l'albergo alpino Steinerkogl, ore 3.

ZELLBERG F 11

Comune, Distretto di Schwaz, abitanti: 650, altezza s.l.m.: 580-1000 m, CAP: 6280. **Informazioni:** Tourismusverband (Associazione Turistica) Zell – Gerlos. Per ulteriori informazioni v. Zell am Ziller.

Il villaggi sparsi di Zellberg costituivano una circoscrizione di Zell, sede del tribunale pupillare di Salisburgo che, tuttavia, dal punto di vista ecclesiastico, appartenne ed appartiene tuttora alla parrocchia di Hippach dato che il torrente Ziller costituisce il confine diocesano e parrocchiale.

Le nuove tecnologie per orientarsi all'aperto necessitano di strumenti di navigazione appropriati e innovativi. I sistemi che si avvalgono della tecnologia **GPS** (Global Positioning System – Sistema di Posizionamento Globale), permettono di localizzare la propria posizione (indicata con coordinate) in tutto il mondo grazie a satelliti che orbitano attorno alla terra ad una distanza di ca. 20.200 Km e ad una velocità di ca. 11.200 km/h emettendo segnali pressochè continui. Se si utilizza l'apparecchio GPS bisogna selezionare con cura i dati del Map Datum ed il relativo ellissoide di riferimento dello Stato in cui ci si trova, evitando così di compromettere l'esattezza delle coordinate. L'utilizzo dell'apparecchio però richiede un po' di esercizio ed una certa pratica nel saper leggere le carte.

Vista sui ghiacciai di Hintertux e la Eggalm
Wandern mit Blick auf den Hintertuxer Gletscher und das Wandergebiet Eggalm
Hiking with a view of the Hintertux glaciers and the Eggalm Hiking Paradise

Telefonnummern der wichtigsten Alpengasthöfe und Unterkunftshütten
Telephone numbers of major restaurants and huts
Elenco dei numeri telefonici dei più importanti alberghi alpini e rifugi

Tuxer Alpen • Tux Alps • Alpi Tuxer

Astegg   05285/62491
Bergrast   05285/62881
Gschößalm   05285/63467
Gschößwandhaus   05285/62880
Lizumer Hütte   05224/52111 + 05223/56209 + 0664/2308516
Penkenhaus   05285/62732
Penkenjochhaus   05285/63345

Zillertaler Alpen • Zillertal Alps • Alpi Zillertaler

Adlerblick 0664/2000332
Alpenrosehütte   05286/5222
Berliner Hütte   05286/5223 + 0676/7051473
Brandberger Kolmhaus   0650/6290263
Breitlahner   05286/5212
Dominikushütte   05286/5216
Edelhütte   0664/9154851 + 0664/1337511
Friesenberghaus   06415/5031 + 0676/749 75 50
Furtschaglhaus   0676/9579818
Gamshütte   0676/3437741
Geraer Hütte   0676/9610303
Gerlosstein-Berghotel   05282/2419 + 0664/3490349
Grawandhütte   05286/5213
Greizerhütte   0664/1029354
Grüne-Wand-Hütte   0664/4332107
Häusling   05289/212
In der Au   05289/214
Kasseler Hütte   0664/1323514 + 05285/63264
Lacknerbrunn   05285/62966
Max-Hütte   05286/5279 + 05285/64815
Olpererhütte   0664/3706709
Pfitscher-Joch-Haus   0039/0472/630119 (Italien/Italy/Italia)
Plauener Hütte   0650/2250369 + 0650/2250370
Richterhütte   06564/7328 + 0664/3704908
Rosshag   05286/5219
Schwarzensteinhütte   0039/0474/671160 (Italien/Italy/Italia)
Spannagelhaus   05287/87707
Steinerkogl-Berggasthaus   05285/63188
Stilluphaus   05285/62496 + 62692
Tuxer-Joch-Haus   05287/87216
Zittauer Hütte   06564/8262 + 0676/6331745

Alle Angaben ohne Gewähr!
All informations without guarantee!
Informazioni non garantite!

Tourismusverbände und Gemeindeämter
Tourist offices and Town Halls
Elenco delle Associazioni Turistiche e degli uffici comunali

	Telefon	Fax
Brandberg	0 52 85/63 1 85	0 52 85/63 8 44
Finkenberg	0 52 87/85 06	0 52 87/85 08
Gerlos	0 52 82/22 81	0 52 82/22 81-80
Gerlosberg	0 52 82/22 81	0 52 82/22 81-80
Hainzenberg	0 52 82/25 18-0	0 52 82/25 18-18
Hippach	0 52 82/36 30 + 25 93	0 52 82/25 93-10
Mayrhofen	0 52 85/67 60	0 52 85/67 60-33
Ramsau im Zillertal	0 52 82/36 30 + 25 93	0 52 82/25 93-10
Rohrberg	0 52 82/22 81	0 52 82/22 81-80
Schwendau	0 52 82/36 30 + 25 93	0 52 82/25 93-10
Tux	0 52 87/85 06	0 52 87/85 08
Zell am Ziller	0 52 82/22 81	0 52 82/22 81-80
Zellberg	0 52 82/22 81	0 52 82/22 81-80

Alle Angaben ohne Gewähr! • All informations without guarantee!
Informazioni non garantite!

Alpine Notrufnummern • Telefono soccorso alpino
Alpine Emergency Telephone Numbers

Europaweit/Per tutta l'Europa/Europe-wide	112
Italien/Italia/Italy	118
Österreich/Austria/Austria	140

andern – Fitness für Körper, Geist und Seele

Zeiten in denen Wandern als langweiliger Rentnersport galt, sind endgültig
bei. Wandern ist in und liegt voll im Trend. Gerade unter jungen Menschen findet
wohl älteste Ausdauersportart immer mehr Fans. Denn abseits vom Arbeitsalltag
en die Menschen verstärkt das Bedürfnis nach körperlicher Betätigung und Be-
gung in der freien Natur. Ob allein oder in der Gruppe, auf einfachen Wegen oder
pruchsvollen Bergrouten – wenn Tourenziel, Können und die Ausrüstung aufeinan-
er abgestimmt sind, wird jede Tour zu einem einzigartigen Naturerlebnis. Und
z nebenbei werden die Ausdauer und das Herz-Kreislaufsystem trainiert.

r sich richtig vorbereitet und kleine Regeln befolgt, kann den Ausflug in die
ur in vollen Zügen genießen und tut gleichzeitig viel für seine Gesundheit.
nützlichen Gesundheits-Tipps von ratiopharm in diesem Lexikon sollen Ihnen
ei helfen.

ste Hilfe für unterwegs

für eine Erstversorgung vor Ort ausgerüstet zu sein, darf eine Wanderapotheke
einem Rucksack fehlen. ratiopharm, Deutschlands große Gesundheitsmarke,
pfiehlt folgende Grundausstattung:

eft- und Blasenpflaster

terile Wundauflagen und Verbandspäckchen

reieckstuch (als Ersatz können auch Hals- oder Kopftuch fungieren)

elastische Binden zur (Gelenk-) Stabilisierung

eukoplast/Tapeverband

lu-Rettungsdecke

inmalhandschuhe

ieber- und Schmerzmittel: z. B. **Paracetamol-ratiopharm® 500**

Wunddesinfektionsmittel: z. B. **PVP-Jod-ratiopharm® Salbe**

räparat gegen Durchfall: z. B. **Loperamid-ratiopharm® akut**

Medikament bei Kreislaufproblemen: z. B. **Etilefrin-ratiopharm®**

ratiopharm

rin-ratiopharm® Tropfen: Wirkstoff: Etilefrinhydrochlorid Anwendungsgebiete: Kreislaufregulationsstörungen mit zu diedrigem
uck, der im Sehtest mit Beschwerden wie Blässe, Schweißausbruch, Flimmern oder Schwarzwerden vor den Augen sowie mit einem
chen Blutdruckabfall ohne einen Anstieg der Herzschlagrate einhergehen kann. Stand: 1/97 Loperamid-ratiopharm® akut Wirkstoff:
amid Anwendungsgebiete: Behandlung akuter Durchfälle bei Erwachsenen und Kindern ab 12 Jahren, sofern keine kausale Therapie
rfügung steht. Eine über 2 Tage hinausgehende Behandlung darf nur unter ärztlicher Verordnung oder Verlaufsbeobachtung erfolgen
l: 8/02 Paracetamol-ratiopharm® 500 Tabletten: Wirkstoff: Paracetamol Anwendungsgebiete: Leichte bis mäßig starke
erzen. Fieber. Für Kinder ab 6 Jahren, für Jugendliche und Erwachsene Stand: 2/03 PVP-Jod-ratiopharm® Salbe: Wirkstoff:
don-Jod Anwendungsgebiete: Zur wiederholten, zeitlich begrenzten oberflächlichen Anwendung bei Schnitt- und Schürfwunden,
ennungen und Verbrühungen, infizierten und superinfizierten Hauterkrankungen, Druck- und Unterschenkelgeschwüren (Decubitus, Ulcus
Stand: 2/01
siken und Nebenwirkungen lesen Sie die Packungsbeilage und fragen Sie Ihren Arzt oder Apotheker.

Mit ratiopharm gut gerüstet in die Natur!

Wandern an der frischen Luft ist eine Wohltat für Körpe
Geist und Seele. ratiopharm möchte, dass Sie gesund
bleiben und engagiert sich deshalb in der Gesundheits
sorge. Sollten Sie doch einmal Beschwerden haben, ha
wir eine Vielzahl an Arzneimitteln für Sie bereit.
Fragen Sie in Ihrer Apotheke nach ratiopharm.

ratiopha
Gute Preise. Gute Bess

ISB N 978-3-85491-561-4

9 783854 915614

€ 7,95

WK 037